THE COMPLETE ADHD PARENTING GUIDE FOR BOYS

Discover Scientific Strategies to Manage Behavioral
Problems, Improve Social Skills and Ensure School
Success Without Yelling.

QC HARMONY

Download the Audiobook Version for FREE

If you love listening to audiobooks on-the-go, you can download the audiobook version of this book for FREE (Regularly $19.95) just by signing up for a FREE 30-day audible trial!

Click the links below to get started

>> For Audible US <<

>> For Audible UK <<

>> For Audible FR <<

>> For Audible DE <<

>> For Audible CA <<

>> For Audible AU <<

CONTENTS

Introduction   1

1. Get Started with Understanding ADHD   6

    Case Study: The Story of Ethan

    Understanding ADHD

    What are the Signs of ADHD?

    What Causes ADHD?

    Importance of a Positive and Supportive Approach

    How Can Parents Help?

    Build a Collaborative Network

    Chapter Takeaway

2. Recognize the Different ADHD Types   23

    Case Study: Max

    Types

    Inattention

    Hyperactive

    Combined-Type

    How is ADHD in Boys Different from Girls?

    Chapter Takeaway

3. How ADHD Treatment in Childhood Works- Understand the Strategies   37

    Case Study

    Diagnosis

    Medicine

Therapy

Tips for Parents

Chapter Takeaway

4. Full Guide to Behavioral Resilience and Effective Behavioral   49
    Management

    Case Study

    Positive Reinforcement Techniques

    Creating a Structured Environment for a Child with ADHD

    Behavioral Charts and Tokens

    Preschoolers (Age 5 and Younger)

    Children Ages 6-12

    Teens

    Model Positive Behavior

    Chapter Takeaway

5. How to Unlock Potential by Using Effective Techniques for   64
    School Success

    Case Study

    Recognizing and Addressing Academic Challenges

    Setting Up Your Child For School Success

    Structured Routine

    Active Learning Techniques

    Ways To Help Your Child with Homework

    Educational Rights

    Chapter Takeaway

6. Build Bridges, Foster Social Growth, and Help Your Boy   79
    Thrive Amidst Peers

    Case Study

    Breaking Down Social Behaviors

    How to Improve Social Skills in Children with ADHD

    Active Listening

Empathy

Set Up Social Goals

Building and Nurturing Friendships

Chapter Takeaway

7. The Roadmap to Executive Functioning and Skills   90
    Development

    Case Study

    Executive Functioning and ADHD

    Effective Communication

    Problem-Solving Skills

    Organizational Skills

    Time Management

    Emotional Regulation

    Chapter Takeaway

8. Navigate the Storm: Strategies for Handling ADHD   109
    Meltdowns and Tough Days

    Case Study

    Tantrums and ADHD

    Why Do Tantrums Occur

    Behavioral Problems Associated with ADHD

    How to Handle Tantrums

    Preventing Tantrums

    Self-Regulation Training

    Chapter Takeaway

9. Master the importance of Clarity and Setting Simple Rules 122

    Case Study

    Be Specific

    Establish Clear Consequences

    Avoid Approaching The Situation With Anger

    Areas to Avoid

Chapter Takeaway

10. How to Use Behavioral Interventions for Long lasting   135
    Success
       Case Study
       Behavioral Therapy
       Parent Training Programs
       Cognitive Behavioral Therapy (CBT)
       Environmental Modifications
       Mindfulness and Relaxation Techniques
       Chapter Takeaway

11. Proven Strategies to Wade the Waters with Your Teenager   147
       Case Study
       Hormonal Changes and ADHD Symptoms
       Emotional Regulation and Mood Swings
       Increased Independence and Responsibility
       Risk-Taking Behavior and Impulsivity
       Parent-Adolescent Relationship
       Chapter Takeaway

12. How to Optimize Physical Activities and Simple Exercises for   159
    Your Child
       Case Study
       Exercise and the Brain
       More Reasons to Exercise
       Easy Exercise Ideas for Kids with ADHD
       Get Out of the House
       How to Help Children With ADHD Sleep
       Chapter Takeaway

13. Learn to Stay Healthy, Positive, and Relentless   172
       Case Study
       Stay Positive

Self-Care

Stay Organized

Develop Coping Strategies

Establish Structure and Stick To It

Celebrate Progress

Chapter Takeaway

Conclusion   186

YOUR FREE GIFT   191

THANK YOU   193

REFERENCES   195

INTRODUCTION

Kids do well if they can. If they aren't doing well, it means there's a barrier between effort and success that must be addressed.

– Dr. Ross Greene

Do you know that many folks believe that people with ADHD have superpowers? They think it's an unfair advantage because of the benefits that come with having this condition. The combination of hypersensitivity, hyperactivity, and hyperfocus can make anyone stand out, so much so that people would say your kid has an unfair advantage.

I've never been one to believe that people with ADHD have difficulty focusing completely. The numerous research studies in support of hyperfocus back me up on this. They may not be able to focus on many things, but they can focus on a few things that catch their interest. Michael Jordan, for example, went on to become arguably the greatest basketball player of all time, demonstrating that individuals with ADHD can achieve remarkable success in their chosen fields. Emma Watson (Hermione in the Harry Potter series) also lives with ADHD, but she played her part so brilliantly as a kid actress and continues to impact the world today. The fact is that ADHD kids have many advantages that their neurotypical counterparts don't have. Say your ADHD boy loves science experiments; for example, if you learn the right techniques and can zoom in on this interest of his, we might be looking at the next genius scientist in the making. Why? He won't get tired as easily as his friends and will most likely see things they don't due to his great focus strength.

It's 100% true that whatever your boy loves or has developed an interest in right now is not the only thing that's important in his life. He also has to succeed at school, obey rules at home, make friends, regulate his emotions, stay healthy, and fulfill many other expectations. But let's start from the known. Your boy will do all that's expected of him if *you* understand and show that you do.

Seeing your boy's condition (I'd rather use the word 'superpower') as a problem will create a rift that'll be difficult to bridge. But if you just take some time to see, to really see how you can make this ADHD work to your advantage, then maybe your boy will make you proud, more than you've imagined, while he's also brilliantly keeping up with the other aspects of his life.

Parenting a boy brings a lot of joy and a heap of frustration. The overflowing toy bins are accompanied by endless questions that might make you feel dizzy: Why is the sky blue? How do airplanes fly? Can fish breathe underwater? It's a whirlwind of "whys" and "hows" and your ever-expanding vocabulary of "I don't know."

As for parenting an ADHD boy, it's all of the above but with triple more energy. Mornings with ADHD might mean missing shoes, forgotten lunches, and huge tantrums over misplaced socks. It's not laziness or defiance; your boy simply has a mind that races ahead of itself, making it difficult to prioritize and remember small details. Executive functioning, planning, and organization are usually a big issue for kids with ADHD. This also affects their social interactions as their impulsiveness and emotional intensity might often be misinterpreted, leading to misunderstanding and frustration. They may also not gain friends easily; if they do, they often lose them too fast.

The average age for an ADHD diagnosis is seven, but children with more severe ADHD can often be identified at a younger age (CDC 2024). An estimated 9.8% (almost 6 million) of U.S. children aged 3 to 17 have ever been diagnosed with ADHD, compared to 8.7% (more than 5 million) of U.S. children who are currently diagnosed with ADHD. Imagine 6 million kids, a whole stadium full of bouncing energy, all with ADHD. That's roughly how many children have been diagnosed with this condition. In the United States, boys are more frequently than girls to be diagnosed with ADHD, with around 11.9% of boys aged 3 to 17 years being diagnosed, compared to 5.5% of girls (Bitsko *et al.,* 2019).

Overwhelming but not without hope. This book will teach you how to hone the benefits of ADHD while nicely trimming away the excesses that translate to constant headaches for you. I'll show you how to organize your child for maximum success and take it one day at a time without losing hope. I've been where you are, staring down a mountain of information and feeling lost. I've pulled through, and I can help you do likewise. I'm here to help you overcome the obstacles and embrace your child's peculiarities.

With a special education and counseling background, I have spent years in school and community organizations, advocating for neurodiversity and inclusive education. Raising a son diagnosed with both ADHD and autism was a tough one. I had too many unexpected twists and turns trying to understand and meet his specific needs.

Seeing the information gap, I knew I had to act. This book is the outcome of that journey, combining my professional knowledge with the honest, sometimes messy realities of parenthood. It is a guide, a companion, and a source of hope for parents whose boys have been diagnosed with ADHD. I will show you practical ways to deal with the meltdowns, improve communication, channel your boy's energy to the right things, and ultimately stand through whatever might accompany this diagnosis. I will also share stories of real parents going through similar challenges and how they're handling things.

This book is about more than just dealing with the mayhem. I will help you see what lies ahead and within the whirlwind. You'll learn to deal with the special joys and challenges of raising a boy with ADHD. I will show you how you can embrace the differences, master them, and also bridge the gap between his world and yours.

The chapters of this book are focused on teaching you to navigate the ADHD journey effectively as a parent, how to recognize the type of ADHD your son has, the best treatment options, and the nuances of behavioral management. We will also discuss how to unlock your kid's potential for school success, help him foster social growth, and best strategies for activating his executive functioning. Everything about navigating the dark days, organizing your son's space to set clear expectations, and many more exciting topics will be covered. There are a whole lot of tips for you, even if your son is already a teenager and needs help navigating his ADHD. Then, of course, we'll take a look at you and how *you* can stay positive through all of these.

You'll learn to spot the master mind hiding in the cluttered room, the inventor behind the misplaced homework, and the artist behind the misplaced gloves. You'll learn to channel his energy, direct his creativity, and lay a solid foundation of support and structure that will allow him to flourish.

This is messy, honest, and the ultimate guide for the mom or dad who feels lost in the chaos of raising your special son.

This is your cue to keep reading to uncover all the findings I've put together and how they can help your son hone his 'unfair' advantage.

1

GET STARTED WITH UNDERSTANDING ADHD

Understanding is the first step to acceptance, and only with acceptance can there be recovery.

J.K. Rowling

A parent of an ADHD kid can at first be very disoriented at the news of the diagnosis. It's difficult to accept, especially if one isn't familiar with the condition. But you don't have to despair because you're about to understand what ADHD is all about.

This chapter will explain the meaning of ADHD, its causes, and its signs. We'll also dispel myths and misconceptions and understand how parents can help while building a collaborative network to make the work easier. Let's get right in.

Case Study: The Story of Ethan

My son came into the world without a sound. He looked perfect on the day he was born, with bright, curious eyes that scanned the room, soaking in every detail. My wife and I named him Ethan, which means "solid," because I wanted him to be strong and solid like my dad, his grandfather. As I held him for the first time, I felt grateful to be the father of such a perfect little wonder.

Years went by quickly, and I watched with dismay as Ethan grew from the adorable little baby in the delivery room to a boy with major developmental problems. He would hit his friends just to show them he was happy, regardless of how often we cautioned him not to.

I clearly remember the evening when my wife patiently explained the concept of death to Ethan. Once she finished, she asked if he had any questions. To which Ethan replied, "Did you ever die?" Despite this incident, my wife and I were in denial about the severity of Ethan's developmental delays until a doctor confirmed, "He's years behind where he should be." I went from dreaming about paying for Ethan's Harvard education to watching him climb aboard the special education bus each morning. Though we couldn't deny that Ethan was different from other kids, I was determined to make him "normal" if I tried hard enough.

When Ethan was six years old, he joined a T-ball league, but he was more interested in collecting dandelions than playing the game. He couldn't understand why his teammates were running around trying to catch a ball when there were so many beautiful flowers to gather.

By the time he was seven, he was diagnosed with attention deficit hyperactivity disorder (ADHD), and his unusual behavior continued. But I was determined to find something he could enjoy like any other little boy. So, I signed him up for Boy Scouts and even volunteered to be the troop leader.

We started with a series of weekend hikes. Halfway through each expedition, I found myself carrying Ethan's backpack and my own as he would stop to look for anthills or trace pictures in the dirt with a stick.

Sitting there under the scorching sun, I felt more frustrated than ever. Ethan, however, seemed oblivious to my disappointment and was busy looking for fish in the lakes along the trail. I couldn't help but wonder why he couldn't be like any other boy who could paddle a canoe, score a goal, or hit a home run. I was

obsessed with having a son like everyone else's. But then, I started to ask myself.
What was I doing? I realized it didn't matter if Ethan wasn't interested
in hitting a home run or being the fastest down the river. He was too busy
discovering the world around him. I finally understood that Ethan was not the
perfect little boy I had hoped for in the hospital long ago, but he was happy.
Ethan pointed at a butterfly that had perched atop his shoe and gave me a big
smile, and that's when it hit me - Ethan was content with the simple things in
life, and that's all that mattered.

During camp that evening, he locked his arms around me, looked into my eyes,
and said, "This is the best trip ever!" At that moment, for the first time in a
long time, I felt lucky to be Ethan's father.

Understanding ADHD

Almost every child has times when their actions go out of control. It's not
unusual for your kid to be in constant motion, shout at the top of their
lungs, and refuse to wait their turn. They may even crash into everything
around them, and at other times, they drift as if in a daydream, unable to pay
attention or finish what they start. However, for some kids, these kinds of
actions might be an indication of something major. Children with attention
deficit hyperactivity disorder (ADHD) show frequent and severe behavioral
issues that affect their ability to live a regular life.

ADHD is a chronic neurological disorder that impairs children's ability
to manage their behavior. This condition has some particular behavioral
patterns. For example, children with ADHD usually struggle to get along
with their siblings at home and other children in school. This difficulty in
paying attention can ripple into their performance at school. An impulsive
nature can also put them in danger. Imagine an impulsive child trying to
cross the road alone; dangerous, right? If left untreated, ADHD can cause

major, lifetime issues, such as low grades in school, run-ins with the law, unsuccessful relationships, and inability to hold a job.

ADHD is now one of the most extensively studied childhood competitions. Current research suggests that several factors may contribute to ADHD. Differences in brain anatomy and function, particularly lower activity levels in areas controlling attention and activity, are associated with ADHD (Hoge *et al.*, 2017). In addition, ADHD has been shown to be linked to genetics, with ADHD often running in families, presenting a 1 in 4 chance for a child with ADHD to have a parent with the condition.

Causes

- Head injuries

- Prematurity

- Prenatal exposures, such as alcohol or nicotine, also heighten the risk of developing ADHD.

- In rare cases, exposure to environmental toxins, like lead during pregnancy, can impact child development.

Myths and misconceptions

Notably, there is no evidence linking ADHD to factors such as excessive sugar consumption, food additives, allergies, or immunizations.

There has been groundbreaking research shedding light on this condition. However, there are still many myths surrounding ADHD; this may lead to misinformation, making it even harder to deal with the twists surrounding the disorder.

- **ADHD kids are lazy**

One popular myth is that children with ADHD simply need to try harder. ADHD is not a matter of motivation or laziness. Children with ADHD usually put in more effort to stay focused. Instructing a child with ADHD to "just focus" is like expecting a nearsighted person to just see farther.

- **ADHD kids can never concentrate**

Another myth is that kids with ADHD can never concentrate. While staying focused is a big challenge for ADHD kids, they can intensely focus on things they find interesting, termed hyperfocus. Math class might be a struggle, but the same child can be a master at building Legos or focusing on whatever game they find amusing.

- **All ADHD kids are hyperactive**

It is also not true that all kids with ADHD are hyperactive. The stereotype of hyperactive kids running around does not apply to every child with ADHD. There are three types of ADHD, and one of them (ADD) does not significantly impact activity levels; it mainly affects attention. While some symptoms may lessen or change with age, most children with ADHD do not completely outgrow it. The symptoms can degenerate in adulthood, especially when left untreated. That is why getting a diagnosis and a plan to manage the disorder is important. Do not just leave your boy to chance.

What are the Signs of ADHD?

Spotting signs of ADHD in kids is like finding little clues that show you how their brain works.

- **Difficulty in paying attention**

One of the first signs you are likely to notice is that they find it difficult to sustain attention. When you force your boy to do addition and subtraction, he looks like he is daydreaming. He may also miss out on details and make mistakes while carrying out tasks that require focus.

- **Hyperactivity**

Next is hyperactivity. Boys are usually a bundle of energy, but hyperactive kids are always in a frenzy. He is moving so fast you feel dizzy just watching him move around. He cannot sit still; he has a propensity to fidget. Short attention spans are also a common trait. Imagine trying to read a book, but your mind keeps wandering off, like switching channels on a TV without warning. This makes it hard for him to follow instructions or complete tasks that he needs to focus on for a long period of time. Please note that this is not a conscious choice or a lack of interest; it is just a manifestation of how their brain processes information.

Another offshoot of your boy's rapid pace of thought is the tendency to make careless mistakes. In class, this can translate into missing steps while solving a math problem or forgetting the alphabet while spelling. This mistake is not because your child is negligent but because he has a racing mind, which makes it difficult to check details meticulously.

- **Constant Fidgeting**

Constant fidgeting involves persistent and often involuntary restlessness, where your child frequently shifts positions, taps his or her feet, or plays with objects. This is due to excess energy and a natural inclination to move. A child with ADHD who is always fidgeting would find it hard to concentrate in class and sit still. Again, it is not a sign of disinterest or intentional disruption but reflects their difficulties in sitting still.

- **Struggling to fall or stay asleep**

Many children with ADHD struggle to fall asleep and stay asleep, leading to chronic fatigue and increased difficulty focusing during the day. This can be a vicious cycle, impacting both focus and sleep quality. While not inherent to ADHD, some kids may show impulsive or aggressive behavior, especially when frustrated or overwhelmed.

- **Experiencing bullying or becoming bullies**

Another telltale sign is that children with ADHD can be prone to both bullying and being bullies themselves. This impulsivity and social challenges can make them vulnerable to manipulation or aggression from others, while their negativity can make them lash out at others. The constant need for attention, often misinterpreted as "acting out," can stem from a genuine desire for connection and validation. These children may struggle with social cues and communication, making it harder to build fulfilling relationships.

- **Loneliness**

Despite craving the attention of their parents and loved ones, children with ADHD often experience loneliness. Difficulty understanding social cues and handling relationships can make them feel isolated. You can help by encouraging peer-to-peer interactions in the right environment to bridge the gap and combat the feelings of isolation.

- **Stubbornness and people-pleasing**

The pendulum of stubbornness and people-pleasing can swing both ways in children with ADHD. In some situations, they may be strong-willed and inflexible; in others, they may become overly compliant and struggle to assert their own needs. You need to understand the reasons behind these behaviors and give them gentle guidance while helping them set healthy boundaries.

What Causes ADHD?

I glazed over the causes of ADHD earlier, but allow me to explain even further in the next couple of paragraphs.

- **Family history**

Just like having brown eyes or curly hair, your boy has a higher chance of developing ADHD if there is a family history of the disorder. This does not mean it is guaranteed, but it is more likely if someone in the family has it. Research shows that about one in four kids with ADHD have a parent with the same condition. So, it is like a family trait, but it does not mean everyone in the family will have it.

- **Exposure to environmental toxins**

Also, exposure to environmental toxins during pregnancy has been shown to increase the likelihood of having a child with ADHD. Harmful substances like lead or toxins in what you eat, drink, or breathe, can leave a mark on the growing brain, affecting how it works. Thankfully, this is not very common, but it is important to consider.

- **Mother's activity during pregnancy**

What a mother does during pregnancy can significantly affect the physical and mental development of a child. If a mother uses certain drugs while pregnant, it can impact the baby's brain development. The baby's brain is still in the making, and any disturbances during this crucial time can affect how it functions. It is important to take good care of yourself during pregnancy to help your little one's brain grow healthy.

- **Premature birth**

Sometimes, babies decide to come into the world a bit earlier than expected. When a baby is born before it is fully ready, it might increase the chances of ADHD. Premature birth can bring its own set of challenges, and one of them might be a higher likelihood of ADHD. You can picture it as the brain being on a developmental schedule and this schedule getting disrupted when the baby is born prematurely.

Importance of a Positive and Supportive Approach

- **Improved adaptive functioning**

A positive and supportive approach is integral to the holistic well-being of children with ADHD. It goes beyond mere symptom management; you have to incorporate developing essential life skills, cultivating positive relationships, and preventing secondary challenges. This is because adopting a positive and supportive approach is important in building adaptive functioning in kids with ADHD. Allow me to break that down. Adaptive functioning is the ability to carry out everyday tasks effectively. Creating a supportive environment can help your kids develop needed life skills like organization, time management, and task completion. This positive reinforcement will help them go through daily challenges more easily, thus improving overall functioning.

- **Reducing behavioral problems**

Another reason you need to be positive and supportive is that being there for your boy reduces behavioral problems associated with ADHD. Acknowledge and understand your child's peculiarities, as this will help you bridge the gap and understand how they feel. Show them how to communicate constructively, set clear expectations, and praise them when they do well. This will significantly reduce the rate of disruptive behavior. That is one step toward beating ADHD.

- **Promoting a positive parent-child relationship**

Amidst of all these, do not lose the chance to bond with your child. Building and maintaining a strong parent-child relationship is indispensable for effective ADHD management. Active listening, open communication, and mutual understanding are all things you need to get conversant with. It might seem overwhelming initially, but I assure you, you will get the hang of it over time. Your relationship with your boy is strengthened when you handle issues associated with ADHD with love, care, and support. This would help you build trust and make it easy for your child to ask for help whenever they need you.

- **Help in managing the symptoms**

The symptoms of ADHD can make you want to tear your hair out, but don't do that. A positive and supportive approach will help you and your son manage the symptoms, reduce tantrums and meltdowns, and have better day-to-day experiences.

- **Preventing or reducing secondary problems such as depression and anxiety disorders**

A downside to ADHD is the rise of secondary issues like anxiety and sadness. Do not worry; this can be well managed by taking a proactive and encouraging approach. The chance of developing other mental health issues is reduced when you are there for your child. This approach helps you acknowledge that your child is going through so much but also helps you see that you can provide so much help by being there for them every step of the way.

How Can Parents Help?

Case Study

Tony looked out the window so his wife would not see his tears. Everyone expected him to be the perfect father, the rock, the man who knew how to fix things. However, today, he felt totally lost and helpless. How could he be the anchor for a child who seemed to exist in an alternate universe? The picture of his son, his eyes wide with frustration, struggling with simple homework, made him sick to the stomach. His anxiety felt like quicksand, threatening to engulf him completely.

However, he wanted to protect him, to fortify himself against the expectations of the outside world. Tony just wanted his boy to be happy and maybe, just maybe, "normal."

- **Be involved**

One of the ways you can really help your boy is to be involved. Not one leg in and another out; be thoroughly involved and immersed in all that pertains to them. You can start by reading extensively and widely on the disorder. Knowledge is power, so get as much information as you need. Read books, talk to doctors and specialists, and connect with other parents. The more you understand your child's unique challenges, the better equipped you will be to support them.

Also, learn to be present when with them. Put down your phone, turn off the TV, and dedicate quality time to your child. Engage in their interests, listen actively, and build a strong, open communication channel. This connection builds a bridge that helps you cross into their world. Structure is a lifesaver for children with ADHD. Consistent schedules, clear expectations, and visual reminders can help them stay on track and feel less overwhelmed.

- **Administer medicines safely**

Work closely with your doctor. Medication has been proven to help manage ADHD symptoms, but you also have to follow the doctor's instructions and monitor any potential side effects. Talk openly and honestly with your child about their medication. Explain its benefits and potential drawbacks, and answer any questions they might have. However, you should also note that medication should complement, not replace, other support strategies like behavior management, therapy, and educational interventions.

- **Work with your child's school**

Build a partnership with your child's teachers and school counselors. Share information about their ADHD diagnosis and collaboratively develop strategies for success in the classroom. Do not hesitate to request accommodations or modifications to help them learn effectively and thrive in school. Attend meetings and parent-teacher conferences, and regularly communicate about your child's progress. It may mean you have to put more items on your to-do list, but it is all part of the demands of being a parent. It is tough, but trust me, it will pay off eventually.

- **Parent with purpose and warmth**

It may be tough but learn to discipline with love. Set clear boundaries and consequences, but always approach your child with understanding and love. They are not being difficult on purpose; their behaviors are often a result of their ADHD. Praise their efforts, celebrate their achievements, and shower them with unconditional love. This positive approach will build their self-esteem and encourage them to keep trying.

- **Connect with others for support and awareness**

Being a parent to a child with ADHD is demanding. Do not neglect your own well-being. Make time for self-care, seek support from your partner and family, and do not be afraid to ask for help when you need it. Trust me, you will need a lot of it. So, please do not be hesitant to ask for help. Connect with other parents who understand your challenges and can offer help and advice and share experiences. This sense of community would be truly helpful.

Build a Collaborative Network

Raising a son with ADHD does not have to be a solo act. Building a strong collaborative network around you and your child can make the process smoother, more effective, and ultimately more joyful for everyone involved. I will show you some key players to bring into your team.

- **Collaborate with school personnel**

Let's start with the teachers. Develop a close relationship with your son's teachers. Share his ADHD diagnosis and discuss specific strategies they can implement in the classroom, like providing clear instructions, offering frequent breaks, and using visual aids.

- **Therapeutic professionals**

It will also do a lot of good if you work with guidance counselors. They are professionals who can give your son the emotional and social support he needs. This would help him manage frustration, build coping mechanisms, and do well in peer relationships. Suppose your son qualifies for an individualized education program (IEP). In that case, the specialist will work with you and the school to develop a tailored plan to address his learning; connecting with other parents who understand the challenges and triumphs of raising a son with ADHD can also help. These groups can be found online, in your community, or you can ask your doctor or therapists. By working together, different professionals can address your son's ADHD from multiple angles, ensuring he receives comprehensive and coordinated care.

A strong network can help distribute the workload and responsibilities, making it less overwhelming for you as a parent. Regular communication between all parties involved in your son's care will also help you better understand and improve strategies and, ultimately, get better outcomes for him. Building a strong network takes time and effort. Do not get discouraged if you don't see immediate results. Keep at it; you will eventually find the right team for your son and family.

Chapter Takeaway

- ADHD is a chronic neurological disorder that impairs children's ability to manage their behavior. This condition has particular behavioral patterns. Children with attention deficit hyperactivity disorder (ADHD) show frequent and severe behavioral issues that affect their ability to live a regular life.

- One of the first signs you are likely to notice is that they find it difficult to sustain attention. Next is hyperactivity. Boys are usually a bundle of energy, but hyperactive kids are always in a frenzy. The tendency to make careless mistakes is another offshoot of your boy's rapid pace of thought.

- Exposure to environmental toxins during pregnancy has been shown to increase the likelihood of having a child with ADHD. Harmful substances like lead or toxins in what you eat, drink, or breathe can leave a mark on the growing brain, affecting how it works.

- Building a strong network takes time and effort. Do not get discouraged if you don't see immediate results. Keep at it; you will eventually find the right team for your son and family.

With a comprehensive understanding of ADHD, you are ready to move on to the next step: recognizing the type of ADHD that your boy is dealing with. We will look at this in the next chapter.

***

Get FREE AUDIOBOOK HERE!

If you scanned the QR code and didn't receive the message, feel free to DM me 'FREE AUDIOBOOK' to get your hands on a free audiobook!

If you're enjoying 'The Complete ADHD Parenting Guide for Boys' so far, I'd be thrilled if you could take a moment to leave a review on Amazon. Your feedback is invaluable! It only takes a minute and would be incredibly valuable for a small independent author like me. Here's the link to leave a review:

US

UK

2

RECOGNIZE THE DIFFERENT ADHD TYPES

ADHD is not a disability; it's a different ability.

- Edward M. Hallowell

ADHD comes in different forms, and these forms impact the exact kinds of symptoms to expect. When you understand the type of ADHD that your boy is dealing with, it'll be easier to apply the right approach and avoid and miss techniques. So let's go into this chapter to understand this crucial subject and see also how ADHD is different in boys and girls.

Case Study: Max

Max's parents and teachers reported that he was having difficulty focusing in class. He often misses instructions, loses track of assignments, and daydreams during lessons. He leaves tasks unfinished, forgets homework, and struggles to organize his belongings. Max also experiences social difficulties. He frequently forgets instructions during games, loses interest in conversations midway, and appears distracted or uninterested. Despite scoring within the average range on standardized tests, Max's grades are inconsistent due to incomplete work and missed deadlines.

Types

ADHD presents in different ways. While the most common and obvious presentation may be hyperactivity and fidgeting, there are other forms of ADHD characterized by struggling with inattention and daydreaming. This makes ADHD less visible and sometimes leads to misdiagnosis and under-support.

- **Predominantly inattentive presentation**

I'll start with the predominantly inattentive presentation. As the name suggests, a child diagnosed with this trait would show signs of gross inattention and consistent distraction. Surprisingly, it is noteworthy that more girls tend to be diagnosed with the inattentive type of ADHD than boys. But it is not totally extinct in boys.

Watch out for instances where your boy may overlook specifics or make oversights. He may also keep making careless mistakes, so be observant of situations where there's a lack of carefulness or attention to detail.

He may also struggle to pay attention and stay on task. Take notes if your boy struggles with maintaining focus and sticking to a task. Also, pay attention to instances where active listening seems challenging for the boy. Unable to follow instructions is another sign of predominantly inattentive presentation. Identify situations where comprehension or adherence to instructions becomes difficult.

You can also check if there's a pattern of avoiding tasks that require a certain level of effort. Look for signs of your boy getting easily distracted in various settings, and also note instances where forgetfulness is a recurring behavior.

You should also monitor situations where essential items are frequently misplaced.

- **Predominantly hyperactive-impulsive presentation**

On the other hand, the predominantly hyperactive-impulsive presentation is usually characterized by fidgeting, squirming, finding it difficult to sit still, running around, climbing chairs, walls, or tables at inappropriate times.

Your boy can also have trouble playing quietly, talking way too much, talking out of turn, blurting out, interrupting, or being constantly "on the go" as if "driven by a motor." Children with hyperactive-impulsive type ADHD can be a disruption in the classroom. They can make learning more difficult for themselves and other students. In this case, more boys are diagnosed with the hyperactive-impulsive type than girls.

Since this is a common trait in boys, I understand that most parents can be skeptical about making decisions based on assumptions and conclusions.

- **Combined presentation**

Some children actually combine both of these classes. This is the most common type of ADHD. Kids with it have symptoms of both inattentive and hyperactive-impulsive types. To be sure, you can take things up with your medical practitioner and use a daily routine that can help.

Inattention

Attention issues are often a problem for ADHD boys, although it's important to note that it's not all attention issues that ADHD causes. Let's take a look at some common ways that attention issues might show up in your boy.

- **Short attention span for their age:**

A lot of kids with ADHD have serious trouble focusing and participating in different activities and social situations. This is more than a passing fancy or sporadic disinterest. Their ongoing struggle to maintain focus for an age-appropriate amount of time frequently results in dissatisfaction and difficulties in their day-to-day lives.

- **Difficulty listening to others**

Because they always seem to want to move on to the next topic or activity, they may have difficulty paying attention to what other people say at different times.

- **Difficulty attending to details**

It's easy for an ADHD kid to lose sight of details and make careless mistakes from time to time. He might mess up his homework and fail tests because of this as he can hardly retain the details about anything.

- **Easily distracted**

The most obvious trait is a reduced capacity for sustained concentration. These kids have trouble staying on task, unlike their peers, who could lose themselves in a project for long stretches of time. Their inability to concentrate and constant switching might have a negative effect on their learning in social and academic contexts.

They could struggle to follow instructions with multiple steps, miss important instructions, or lose track of the current subject in the classroom. This might result in academic gaps, dissatisfaction with homework, and a sense of being behind. Staying focused during activities or chats on the playground can be difficult. They might miss turns, forget rules, or abruptly switch activities, leaving friends feeling confused or excluded.

- **Forgetfulness**

This is to be expected since his attention is literally to and fro. He tends to forget things told to him, parental instructions, details about school, and many others.

Strategies

- **Structured routines**

Supporting a child with ADHD involves using simple and effective strategies that fit into their daily life. One helpful approach is creating structured routines. This involves developing a daily schedule that specifies the times for various tasks, such as playing, eating, and schoolwork. Routines bring predictability, helping the child understand what comes next.

- **Visual schedules**

You can incorporate visual schedules into his daily routine and display charts or pictures that help show the sequence of events in a way that's easier to understand than just words. Think of it as a friendly map that helps them confidently go through the day's routines. This visual support improves comprehension and makes routines more manageable, reducing anxiety and frustration.

- **Break tasks into steps**

Your kid will do much better when you break his tasks into small, manageable steps. For example, if you want your kid to have his bath without throwing tantrums, you could break that down this way:

- Don gets out of his chair

- Don comes with Mom to the bathroom

- Don lets Mom help him shower

- Don wraps himself in a towel

When your son accomplishes steps like this, remember to reward him, even if that's just with a pat on the back. It'll help keep this method working positively.

- **Provide clear instructions**

Yes, it's important to make sure that your instructions are clear, simple, and straightforward; otherwise, he will not get to them at all.

Hyperactive

This involves:

- Fidgeting

- Squirming

- Getting up often when seated

- Running or climbing at inappropriate times

- Having trouble playing quietly

- Talking too much

When compared to their peers, children with ADHD may exhibit a range of hyperactive behaviors that are either more severe or frequent. One common sign is fidgeting, where they may constantly move or squirm, even when expected to remain still.

Another aspect of hyperactivity is the struggle to do things quietly. It might be difficult for kids with ADHD to play quietly, and they could play more loudly and actively than their classmates. Furthermore, excessive chatting is another indicator of hyperactivity. Children diagnosed with ADHD may have a habit of talking too much and frequently cutting other people off in talks.

Strategies

- **Structured physical activities**

Using structured physical activities in your child's routine can be beneficial. These activities can help positively channel your child's energy, reducing restlessness and promoting focus.

- **Frequent breaks**

Frequent breaks are also helpful for children with hyperactivity. Giving them short breaks between tasks allows them to release excess energy, making it easier for them to concentrate when they return to the activity. A quick one here: taking short breaks works for adults, too. Whenever you feel too overwhelmed or choked, you can take a break and come back. Trust me, you'll be more focused by the time you resume what you are doing.

- **Teach self-control techniques**

Teaching your son self-control techniques can also help him manage hyperactivity better. This involves helping him learn how to regulate their impulses and behaviors.

- **Positive reinforcement**

Another thing that really helps is the "thumbs ups," and "good jobs." Recognizing and praising the child for displaying appropriate behavior encourages them to continue making positive choices. It's a way of highlighting their efforts and progress, contributing to their overall development and well-being.

Combined-Type

Symptoms: Children with combined-type ADHD have a distinct set of difficulties due to their combination of hyperactive-impulsive and inattentive symptoms. You need to take these factors into consideration. Adopting effective strategies is needed for their well-being and development.

Diagnosis: You will also need a thorough assessment of the child's behavior to diagnose combined-type ADHD, taking into account both hyperactive-impulsive and inattentive symptoms. Your doctor may need to evaluate the persistence and impact of symptoms on day-to-day functioning or use guidelines like the DSM-5. A diagnosis is usually made based on requirements about the quantity and duration of symptoms.

Strategies

- **Individualized plans**

Every child with combined-type ADHD is unique, so one-size-fits-all solutions won't work. Instead, use personalized plans designed around their strengths, challenges, and how they learn best. These plans might include custom academic support, targeted behavior tools, and strategies to help them improve socially.

- **Collaborate with professionals**

One of the phrases I learned from volunteering in Boy Scouts is "Teamwork Makes the Dream Work." No superhero goes it alone (even Superman eventually needed a Superwoman), and neither should anyone supporting a child with combined-type ADHD. Joining forces with healthcare professionals, educators, and other specialists creates a powerful team for managing this complex condition. Keeping teachers, counselors, and medical professionals in the loop ensures a consistent approach across school, home, and medical settings.

- **Balanced strategies**

It's important to make sure that you're not tipped out of balance while helping your boy. Try to use balanced strategies teaching your boy how to cope in all areas of his life, not just in one area. Keep using these strategies consistently.

How is ADHD in Boys Different from Girls?

Beyond the pink and blues, some things can show up differently depending on whether your child is a boy or a girl. Boys might bounce off the walls, full of energy and impulsive ideas, while girls are more quiet thinkers, easily drifting off in daydreams. Both have ADHD, but the way they show up is different in each gender.

Boys with ADHD often exhibit more overt hyperactivity-impulsivity symptoms, making their challenges more noticeable. They might engage in reckless behaviors, have difficulty playing quietly, and struggle with impulse control. In contrast, girls with ADHD, especially those with a predominantly inattentive presentation, may show internalized symptoms like daydreaming, making it less conspicuous.

Risk factors

Several risk factors contribute to the development of ADHD in both boys and girls. Genetics, for example, have a higher likelihood of ADHD if a close family member has the disorder. Environmental factors, premature birth, low birth weight, and exposure to substances during pregnancy are also associated with an increased risk.

The science behind ADHD in boys

THE COMPLETE ADHD PARENTING GUIDE FOR BOYS   33

Studies using neuroimaging techniques suggest subtle differences in brain structure between boys and girls with ADHD. For example, boys may show atypical activation in the striatum and cerebellum, while girls may exhibit abnormalities in the prefrontal cortex and limbic system (Curatolo et al., 2010).

Brain structure

The brains of boys with ADHD often show structural differences, including alterations in the size and activity of specific brain regions. The prefrontal cortex, responsible for executive functions like impulse control and attention, shows different variances. These structural differences contribute to the challenges in regulating attention and behavior observed in boys with ADHD.

Symptom behavior

Boys with ADHD commonly display symptoms such as impulsivity, hyperactivity, and difficulties sustaining attention. Their behavior may involve constant movement, impulsive decision-making, and difficulty following instructions. Symptoms in boys tend to be more conspicuous, leading to earlier recognition and diagnosis.

Boys are diagnosed with ADHD at significantly higher rates than. This is likely due to the subtle nature of inattentive symptoms in girls, leading to underdiagnosis and undertreatment. Additionally, girls with ADHD are more likely to be diagnosed with comorbid conditions like anxiety and depression.

Chapter Takeaway

- Predominantly hyperactive-impulsive presentation is usually characterized by fidgeting, squirming, difficulty sitting still, running around, and climbing chairs, walls, or tables at inappropriate times.

- Supporting a child with ADHD involves using simple and effective strategies that fit into their daily life. One helpful approach is creating structured routines. This involves developing a daily schedule that specifies the times for various tasks, such as playing, eating, and schoolwork. Routines bring predictability, helping the child understand what comes next.

- Every child with combined-type ADHD is unique, so one-size-fits-all solutions won't work. Instead, use personalized plans designed around their strengths, challenges, and how they learn best. These plans might include custom academic support, targeted behavior tools, and strategies to help them improve socially.

From creating an organized workspace to giving clear instructions and visualization schedules, the different types of ADHD require unique strategies, so ensure you're not approaching your boy with a method that works for another ADHD type. The next chapter will enlighten you further about ADHD treatments and how to choose one for your boy.

***

Get FREE AUDIOBOOK HERE!

If you scanned the QR code and didn't receive the message, feel free to DM me 'FREE AUDIOBOOK' to get your hands on a free audiobook!

I hope you're finding 'The Complete ADHD Parenting Guide for Boys' useful. If so, I would appreciate it if you could leave a review on Amazon to help other parents discover this guide! It only takes a minute and would be incredibly valuable for a small independent author like me. Here's the link to leave a review:

US

UK

3

HOW ADHD TREATMENT IN CHILDHOOD WORKS- UNDERSTAND THE STRATEGIES

"Without knowing the cause of illness, any treatment must be considered a guess."

—— *Richard Diaz*

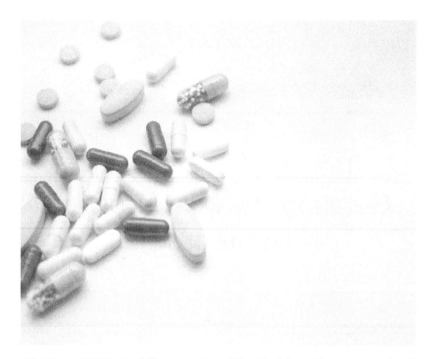

*H*ow ADHD should be treated is still highly debated by many people. The different types of ADHD have different treatments that work best for them, so what works for Child A might not work for Child B.

In this chapter, we'll take a close, careful look at the options available and how to make the best treatment decisions for your child.

Case Study

I was skeptical about medications at first; I didn't know what to expect exactly. Would the pills turn my boy into a glassy-eyed shadow of himself? Every medication has side effects, and I bet this is not exempted. It was a terrifying leap of faith, but watching Tyler struggle, drowning in the chaos of his own mind, was just as unbearable.

The cost was another cause for concern. Could we afford this lifeline, or would it sink us deeper? We took the leap. Tiny orange pills were swallowed with a silent prayer. The first days were initially a blur: sleepy mornings, clumsy stumbles.

I watched with my heart in my throat for something out of place, anything at all.

Gradually, Tyler started to remember to pick up his lunchbox, and he seemed more attentive whenever I spoke to him. His laughter still sounded like fireworks, and he was still so full of energy, but now, there was focus, a steady anchor, keeping him within bounds.

The cost pinched a little, but it paled in comparison to the relief.

Diagnosis

I already mentioned some likely causes of ADHD; let me pitch in one or two more things before I go into symptoms.

Etiology

Deficiencies in essential nutrients like iron, zinc, and omega-3 fatty acids might indirectly contribute to ADHD symptoms by affecting brain function and neurotransmitter synthesis (Millichau et al., 2015). Also, poor sleep quality and chronic sleep deprivation can exacerbate ADHD symptoms due to their impact on attention, cognitive function, and emotional regulation (Cortese et al., 2015).

Surprisingly, recent research suggests that the gut microbiome, comprising various bacterial communities in the digestive system, might be linked to ADHD development and symptom severity. Alterations in gut bacteria composition may influence neurotransmitter signaling and brain function (Huo et al., 2019).

Clinical presentation

Understanding these multifaceted factors does not completely explain a child's ADHD, but it provides a perspective. ADHD manifests uniquely in each child, but recognizing common signs across three main areas can be helpful. So, I created a checklist below to help you mark out your son's symptoms. The more boxes you tick, the more attention you may need to pay to your boy.

Inattention:

- Difficulty focusing on tasks or activities

- Frequent daydreaming or getting lost in thought

- Trouble organizing tasks and completing homework

- Easily distracted by sights and sounds

- Losing things often

- Difficulty remembering instructions

Hyperactivity:

- Constant fidgeting or squirming

- Excessive talking or running around, even in inappropriate settings

- Difficulty sitting still for long periods

- Impulsive behavior, like blurting out answers or taking unnecessary risks

Impulsivity:

- Acting without thinking or considering the consequences

- Difficulty taking turns or waiting patiently

- Interrupting others or blurting out answers

- Engaging in risky or dangerous behaviors

It is important to remember that not all children will display every one of these symptoms; they are only suggestive. The degree of the symptoms can also differ greatly. For an appropriate diagnosis, I would suggest that you go for a professional examination in addition to this, especially if concerns are raised about a child's behavior.

Evaluation

When a child exhibits symptoms of ADHD, the next course of action is to have them professionally evaluated. This usually entails consulting a physician, child psychiatrist, or psychologist. This thorough procedure could entail the following:

1. Clinical Interview: A detailed conversation about the child's development, behavior, and family history.

2. Standardized Tests: Assessment of various cognitive skills, including attention, memory, and executive functioning.

3. Physical Examination: Ruling out underlying medical conditions that could mimic ADHD symptoms.

Medicine

Your son's doctor may recommend some of these medications to help manage the symptoms of ADHD. Each medication has unique features, so reviewing its benefits and potential side effects can prepare you better if needed.

- **Methylphenidate**

Let me start with methylphenidate, found in medications like Ritalin, Concerta, and Focalin, and is quickly absorbed from the stomach, peaking in the bloodstream within 1-2 hours. It requires multiple daily doses with a short half-life of 2-3 hours. Unregulated production of dopamine and norepinephrine is usually the culprit for your child's excessive jumpy behavior. This medication works by blocking the reuptake of dopamine and norepinephrine in the brain, enhancing focus and attention. Common side effects include loss of appetite, insomnia, and headaches. Notably, both children and adults can use methylphenidate, just that the formulations and dosages are different.

- **Lisdexamfetamine**

Lisdexamfetamine, known as Vyvanse, is a prodrug of dextroamphetamine. It undergoes conversion to its active form in the bloodstream, providing a slow and sustained release for up to 12 hours, requiring only a single daily dose. Like methylphenidate, it increases dopamine and norepinephrine levels, improving attention and impulse control. Side effects are similar, with reports suggesting a potentially lower rate of insomnia and decreased appetite. Vyvanse's notable feature is its long-acting effectiveness, which can be quite helpful if your son is not a fan of taking drugs.

- **Dextroamfetamine**

Found in medications like Adderall and Dexedrine, dextroamfetamine is rapidly absorbed from the stomach, reaching peak levels in 1-3 hours. A shorter half-life of 4-10 hours typically necessitates multiple daily doses. Its mechanism of action is like that of methylphenidate and lisdexamfetamine, increasing dopamine and norepinephrine levels to enhance focus and attention. Side effects align with other stimulants, with a notable higher risk of misuse due to its short-acting nature. Despite the risk, it remains effective for both children and adults.

- **Atomoxetine**

Atomoxetine, available as Strattera, is well-absorbed from the stomach, reaching peak levels at 1-4 hours. It boasts a longer half-life (5-10 hours) than stimulants, allowing for a single daily dose. Unlike stimulants, atomoxetine primarily acts as a norepinephrine reuptake inhibitor, influencing attention and impulse control through different mechanisms. While its side effects, including drowsiness and decreased appetite, are less common than stimulants, it offers a non-stimulant alternative, preferred by those concerned about stimulant-related issues.

- **Guanfacine**

The last medication I would be touching on is guanfacine, found in Intuniv, and is well-absorbed from the stomach, peaking at 1-4 hours, with a long half-life of 17 hours, facilitating a single daily dose. Acting as a selective alpha-2A adrenergic receptor agonist, it decreases prefrontal cortex neuronal activity, improving impulse control and attention without directly impacting dopamine or norepinephrine. Side effects, including drowsiness and headaches, are generally well-tolerated. Intuniv is a notable non-stimulant option, particularly effective for managing impulsivity and hyperactivity, with a slower onset of action than stimulants.

I know that looks a bit technical, but taking the time to read up on these medications can help you better deal with the disorder. Understanding how each drug works, its benefits and possible side effects can help you make informed decisions about your child's ADHD treatment. It also allows you to actively engage in discussions with your healthcare provider, ensuring a collaborative approach in tailoring your child's most effective and well-tolerated medication plan.

Therapy

Treating ADHD with medication alone is like trying to sprint a marathon on one leg - you might get a short burst of adrenaline at first, but sooner or later, you will topple over. Therapy strengthens coping skills, builds organizational strategies, and helps your child improve socially.

- **Psychoeducation**

A psycho-educational approach helps in symptom recognition, active participation in treatment, and enhanced adherence to both pharmacological and non-pharmacological interventions for your child's ADHD. Increased awareness of ADHD would help you support your children in reaching their full potential and even help you bond better.

- **Behavior therapy**

Behavior therapy, recognized as effective for ADHD, enhances a child's behavior, self-control, and self-esteem. Particularly impactful when delivered by parents, experts recommend referring parents of children under 12 for behavior therapy training. For those under 6, you can try behavior management training before considering medication. Trained parents acquire skills and strategies to support their child's success in various settings, offering lasting benefits for the child and the family.

- **Training and education programs for parents**

You can also try parent training and education programs designed to help parents learn strategies to improve their kids' behavior. These programs are tailored to fit the family's needs and cover areas like creating house rules, using clear instructions, and using charts, rewards, and consequences. For older kids, the focus tends to shift to consequences like loss of privileges or more chores.

- **Social skills training**

Social skills can be developed even for children with ADHD. This involves acknowledging negative feelings and celebrating success. Role-playing can also help teach children how to behave in certain situations. You can guide them through these scenarios, reinforcing positive social behavior and emotional regulation.

- **Cognitive behavioral therapy**

CBT is becoming increasingly popular for managing ADHD, and it focuses on how thoughts affect behavior and emotions. It can be a major supplement to medication or even an alternative. In children, CBT teaches coping strategies and skills for self-regulation, helping manage emotions and tasks. For adults, CBT aids in managing common ADHD symptoms, offering skills in time management, organizational abilities, and self-regulation. While medication provides immediate relief, CBT instills skills that last a lifetime.

Tips for Parents

Before I wrap up this chapter, let me add some tips to make these a bit easier.

- **Establish a schedule**

Something that can be really useful for kids with ADHD is a routine. Establish a clear schedule for meals, bedtime, homework, and play. Regularity provides a calming framework, reducing anxiety and improving focus. There might be tantrums in the first few days, but stick with your guns, and the routine will soon be established. With it, your kid will know what to expect at different times of the day.

- **Become structured**

Create a dedicated workspace for homework or quiet activities, free from TV blares or sibling chatter. Earphones with calming music can also work wonders. Ensure you also talk clearly and concisely. Instead of vague instructions, give step-by-step breakdowns. Use timers and visual aids to reinforce expectations.

- **Control outside distractions**

Screen time and other outside distractions can make paying attention even more difficult for your boy. It'll be helpful to minimize these as much as you can.

- **Minimize options**

Offer limited options for clothing, snacks, or activities. A smaller selection means less decision fatigue, smoother transitions, and less stress for you.

- **In your conversations with your child, be precise and explicit**

When you know what you're going to tell your child, be ready to be specific and explicit. This means you should be comfortable answering his questions and explaining why he can or cannot do some things.

Chapter Takeaway

- Understanding these multifaceted factors does not completely explain a child's ADHD, but it provides a perspective. ADHD manifests uniquely in each child, but recognizing common signs across three main areas can be helpful.

- Your son's doctor may recommend some medications to help manage the symptoms of ADHD. Each medication has unique features, so reviewing its benefits and potential side effects can prepare you better in case you need them.

- Treating ADHD with medication alone is like trying to sprint a marathon on one leg - you might get a short burst of adrenaline at first, but sooner or later, you will topple over. Therapy strengthens coping skills, builds organizational strategies, and helps your child improve socially.

ADHD does not have a one-size-fits-all treatment, so it's important to remember what was discussed in this chapter. Next, we'll examine how to administer behavioral management when dealing with ADHD in your boy.

***

Get FREE AUDIOBOOK HERE!

If you scanned the QR code and didn't receive the message, feel free to DM me 'FREE AUDIOBOOK' to get your hands on a free audiobook!

Liking the book? Your reviews help tremendously! Please consider sharing your thoughts on Amazon if 'The Complete ADHD Parenting Guide for Boys' has been helpful to you. It only takes a minute and would be incredibly valuable for a small-independent author like me. Here's the link to leave a review:

US

UK

4

Full Guide to Behavioral Resilience and Effective Behavioral Management

---

"If you want to change attitudes, start with a change in behavior."

William Glasser

Using medicines alone to treat ADHD is a terrible idea. It's like you're trying to cut down a tree and instead of going to the roots, you concentrate on the branches. Using behavioral management skills is an integral part of helping your ADHD boy and that's what we'll look at in this chapter.

Case Study

I first came across behavioral management in a pamphlet I picked up at the hospital while Ted and I were waiting to see his doctor. I initially had doubts because I didn't know what to expect; I wasn't even sure if I could pull it off. But I tried, and I'm glad I did.

Managing my boy's impulsiveness was quite challenging, but it was rewarding. We both worked through his high energy levels, impulsivity, and difficulty focusing. Eventually, I was able to help channel his energy into gardening, and now, I have a yard full of roses and hibiscus to show for it.

Positive Reinforcement Techniques

A pat on the back, a compliment, or a thank you note is bound to boost your morale and make you want to do more. In the same way, positive reinforcement can significantly shape your son's behavior and response. With positive reinforcement, you strengthen desired behavior by following them with something pleasant or rewarding. That includes saying "Yay!" or giving a high five when your son does something good.

- **Utilize proper forms of operant conditioning**

One of the techniques you can employ is "operant conditioning." Don't worry; it's not as difficult as the word sounds. Operant conditioning is a learning process where behaviors are modified by their consequences. It's like a feedback loop: if a behavior leads to a positive outcome, it's more likely to be repeated; if it leads to a negative outcome, it's less likely to happen again. Let me break down how it works. Operant conditioning usually starts with an antecedent, that is, something happens that sets the stage for the behavior. This could be an external stimulus, like a bell ringing, or an internal state, like feeling hungry.

A behavior usually follows the antecedent- a specific action done in response to the antecedent. This behavior is followed by either a reinforcer (something that increases the likelihood of the behavior happening again) or a punisher (something that decreases the likelihood of the behavior happening again). A reinforcer encourages him to repeat the action, while a punisher discourages him from doing so again.

- **Do not ignore them**

Another way to demonstrate positive reinforcement is to ensure you don't ignore your son. Rather than focusing on undesired behaviors alone, look out for what he does correctly and praise him for it. Recognize his efforts, no matter how small, rather than ignoring them. This approach helps to build your kid's self-esteem and confidence.

- **Be consistent in your expectations**

Train yourself to be consistent with your expectations. Tell your son exactly what you want from him and stay on it until he yields. You can also practice operant conditioning over and over until he begins to respond in a more appropriate manner. When positive behaviors consistently lead to rewards and negative behaviors result in clear consequences or redirection, it helps create a predictable environment, providing the structure and support he needs.

- **Be aware and plan ahead**

Anticipate potential triggers and plan to minimize disruptions. Providing visual schedules, advance notice of changes (can be as simple as pre-informing your son that you plan to change his favorite snack to something more healthy), and incorporating transitional activities can help reduce stressors contributing to undesired behaviors.

- **Use visual aids**

Visual aids are also quite effective, as children usually respond well to visual stimuli. Create visual charts or schedules outlining tasks, goals, and the associated rewards. These cues are tangible reminders of expectations and help your son stay on track with positive behaviors.

Creating a Structured Environment for a Child with ADHD

Creating a structured environment is like building a sturdy tent amidst the chaos in your son's mind. It gives a sense of predictability and calm.

- **Consistent daily routines**

It can be as simple as creating a consistent morning routine. You can make up a wake-up or teeth-brushing song, making each step predictable and fun. This trains his brain to expect and prepare for what is next. Predictability reduces cognitive load and anxiety, allowing your child to direct his energy toward completing tasks rather than being unsure of what to do.

- **Organized spaces**

Having an organized physical space also helps a lot. Clutter and disorganization can overwhelm children with ADHD and hinder their ability to focus. A clean and clear physical environment gives clear visual cues and promotes a sense of control. This would make it easy for them to find their way around the house and reduce the chances of getting worked up over misplaced toys and pencils. You can designate storage bins and shelves for toys, books, and clothes. You can even use a color code if you want—blue shelf for toys, red shelf for books, and white shelf for clothes. Label the shelves clearly with words or pictures.

Ensure you include him and show him where and how you arrange things. Encourage him to pick up his toys and put them on the appropriate shelf when he is done playing with them.

- **Visual schedules**

For visual aids, you can create pictures or symbol-based visual schedules to outline the day's activities. Use timers to signal the transition between tasks. Also, using a reward chart can help you track progress and motivate positive behavior.

- **Flexibility and patience**

I need to say this again: children with ADHD learn and process information differently. Being rigid and inflexible can make things get worse very quickly. Create an atmosphere of understanding and love around him. Be flexible enough to allow your son to adapt at his own pace. Be patient with yourself also. You are a great Mum (or Dad); you can give yourself some grace on your way to perfection. You won't get all the methods and techniques at once, but you will get better with them over time.

Behavioral Charts and Tokens

Your child is a garden full of seeds and seedlings, yet sometimes needs a little extra tending to flourish. Behavioral charts and tokens can be "extra tending" to encourage and shape desired behaviors in children, especially those needing extra support with focus, self-regulation, or learning. A behavioral chart is a type of positive reinforcement to encourage your child to adopt a new behavior. You can give your son a point, sticker, or token whenever he exhibits a desired behavior. When the child saves up a predetermined number of points or tokens, they can exchange it for a prize, a toy, or a treat. This creates motivation and entices the child to strive for rewards. To use a behavioral chart, you need to:

Define Desired Behaviors: Start by clearly stating specific actions that you want your son to do, like finishing homework or washing the dishes.

Create a Visual Chart: Once you do this, create a visual chart. This can be a homemade drawing, a chart from the store, or a list you both come up with. Either way, ensure that what you have is age-appropriate and visually appealing, with clearly marked activities and corresponding rewards.

Assign Points or Tokens: Choose a system that works for you and your child. Points can be earned directly for desired behaviors, while tokens can also be collected and exchanged for rewards later. I particularly love this technique because it worked for my son and gave me a leveraging tool to get him to do what he needed to do. It also allowed us to bond because we spent time together drawing up the list, calculating tokens, and corresponding rewards. I also got to teach him the value of money on some occasions.

Establish Rewards and Track Progress: You can also set up achievable short-term rewards that motivate your child, like extra playtime, choosing a movie, or a special outing. Take time to regularly review the chart with your child, highlighting successes and adjusting the system as needed.

- **Proactive Strategies**

Being proactive helps you take control and manage a situation even before it happens. When your child constantly reacts to situations or scrambles to meet expectations, his confidence erodes, and he may feel easily frustrated. Taking proactive steps helps you build open communication and trust with your child. This makes it easy for your son to discuss what is bothering him, and allows you to deal with what is wrong, and prevents future occurrences.

- **Clear Expectations**

Children with ADHD often thrive on structure and predictability. Establishing clear expectations sets the stage for positive behavior and reduces confusion. This involves keeping the rules simple and age-appropriate and focusing on positive actions. You should also try to explain expectations clearly, calmly, and consistently. Acknowledge and reward adherence to expectations.

- **Behavioral Contracts**

Behavioral contracts are agreements created with your child to outline specific expectations, desired behaviors, and consequences for adherence and non-adherence. Instead of just focusing on what not to do, emphasize the desired behavior. Start small and gradually increase difficulty as your child succeeds. Use clear rewards and consequences. Ensure they are meaningful and directly related to the behavior. Adapt the contract as needed based on progress and changing needs.

- **Teaching Self-Regulation**

Self-regulation is a crucial skill for managing emotions, impulses, and attention. You can help your child develop this skill by helping them identify and label their emotions. You can also teach them to identify solutions to challenges calmly and constructively. Encourage them to use positive affirmations and self-encouragement.

- **Organizational Support**

Help your child develop systems and routines to stay on track by dividing large tasks into smaller, more manageable steps. Make use of planners and organizers. Visual aids can help them track schedules and deadlines. Create consistent routines for morning, bedtime, homework, etc. Explore apps and tools designed for organization and time management.

- **Social Skills Training**

Social skills training can equip them with the tools to navigate social situations effectively and build positive relationships. Practice social skills in safe, controlled environments. Explain the importance of nonverbal communication, like eye contact and body language. Help your son understand how their actions affect others. You can also encourage him to participate in activities that promote positive social interactions.

Preschoolers (Age 5 and Younger)

- **Organize the Day**

Children thrive on predictability and structure. A consistent daily routine provides a predictable framework for managing their busy minds and bodies. Aim for:

Set wake-up and bedtime schedules: Stick to them as closely as possible, even on weekends.

Schedule regular activities: Meals, playtime, learning activities, and outdoor time.

Use visual aids: Create simple charts or picture schedules to help your child understand the day's flow.

Transition smoothly: Use consistent cues (e.g., singing a song, dimming lights) to signal upcoming transitions.

- **Set Rules and Expectations**

Keep rules simple, age-appropriate, and positive. Focus on what they should do instead of just what they shouldn't. For this age bracket, limit the number of rules. Five or six clear rules are enough for this age group. Use pictures or short phrases to make them easily understood. Explain the "why" behind the rules. Connect them to safety, respect, or other positive values. Gently redirect when needed, using positive language.

- **Use Rewards**

Use rewards strategically to encourage good choices and effort, not just perfect results—reward effort, engagement, and following the rules, not just completing tasks perfectly. Young children have short attention spans, so reward them quickly after the desired behavior. Use a mix of tangible (stickers, small toys) and intangible (praise, extra playtime) rewards. Reward the same behavior consistently to solidify the connection.

- **Use a Timer**

Set timers for limited activities. Use them for screen time, playtime, or task completion. Use timers with visual countdown features or alarms. Gradually increase the duration as your child's focus improves. Avoid framing them as punishments but rather as tools for organization and fun.

- **Engage your Child**

Enjoy your little one; don't just supervise; join the fun. Build towers, read stories, or create silly songs together. Active engagement strengthens your bond, and you also show them how to play correctly. Make playtime collaborative. Take turns leading activities, choosing games, or telling stories. This builds social skills and teaches the importance of cooperation.

Children Ages 6-12

- **Explain and Instruct**

You might want to take a slightly different approach with older boys. Children between 6 and 12 are just venturing into the world, experimenting with independence and a thirst for discovery. You can help shape your boys by providing a compass and the confidence and support they need to evolve. Instead of simply demanding obedience, take the time to explain why certain rules and expectations exist. Talk with them, answer their questions honestly (there will be many), and encourage them to think critically. You can tell them to think of all the possible things that can make an airplane fly before explaining how it flies in as basic details as possible (I wish you good luck with that).

- **Make a Discipline Plan**

I made quite a lot of emphasis on rewards, allowing me to tilt toward discipline a bit. Discipline becomes necessary when boundaries are crossed. Establish clear consequences for unacceptable behavior in advance, ensuring they are proportional and age-appropriate. Avoid harsh punishments or shaming, but communicate consequences calmly and consistently. I understand that sometimes, your child's misbehavior and a tough day at work might make you want to yell or lash out at them. In such instances, you can delay discipline until you are more settled. Or better still, have predetermined consequences for certain actions. For example, watching TV after bedtime means he won't have any screen time tomorrow. This creates a structure to your discipline and helps your child weigh the consequences of his actions even before he acts.

- **Walk your Talk**

Children are keen observers. Your actions speak louder than your words. Live by the values you expect them to embrace. Practice honesty, responsibility, kindness, and respect in your interactions with them and others.

Teens

I get several comments from parents about dreading the "teen years." I agree that the teenage years can test all your parenting skills and make you feel like you have been run over by a train. One minute, your adorable little boy is hugging you and telling you, "You are the best dad in the whole wide world," the next, he's locked himself in his room all day just because you told him to take out the trash.

The adolescent brain undergoes significant reorganization, which leads to the development of better reasoning, critical thinking, and problem-solving skills. However, their impulsivity and emotional regulation can remain underdeveloped, leading to risk-taking behavior and seemingly irrational decisions. Why watch a game all night knowing that exams start tomorrow? That's typical teen behavior, right?

- **Involve Your Child**

To help your teen, you may need to replace lectures with open-ended questions and non-judgmental listening. Focus on understanding their perspectives and concerns rather than imposing your views. Acknowledge and validate their feelings, even if they differ from yours. Phrases like, "It sounds like you're feeling..." or "That must be frustrating" shows them that you truly understand their feelings.

Teens love to be involved; you can encourage their input on household rules, activities, and even family decisions within age-appropriate roles. You can also work together to set realistic goals for school, extracurricular activities, and personal development. Allow them to make the bulk of the decisions while you oversee and guide them. Create space for open and honest conversations about their interests, concerns, and dreams. Actively listen, ask open-ended questions, and avoid judging them or forcing your opinion on them.

- **Discipline in Private**

One thing that causes friction between parents and teens is discipline. How and where you discipline your teen matters as much as the discipline itself. Address any issues privately and calmly. Focus on understanding their perspective and explaining the consequences of their actions. Shouting or public reprimands are likely to be counterproductive and escalate the situation. Try not to bring up past mistakes repeatedly (no one likes to be reminded of their wrongs over and over again). Instead, help them see that they can do better. Reinforce their strengths and let them know you are there to support them to be even much better.

- **Set a Good Example**

Teenagers see and observe things keenly, and they just might call you out on your misbehavior when you try to correct them on the same thing. Practice the values you want them to learn. Setting a good example also means discussing your own values and decision-making process. Tell them why you would rather save than get another pair of heels. Share your struggles and experiences, too; the more you share, the more likely they are to share with you.

Be a lifelong learner and role model positive personal growth. Be open to correction, and don't hesitate to apologize when you are wrong. It may not be easy at times, but I assure you, it is all for good.

Model Positive Behavior

Children are like sponges, soaking up everything they see and experience. While lectures and instructions hold value, modeling positive behavior is the most powerful tool in shaping who they become.

- **Stay Calm and Patient**

Children naturally test boundaries and push limits. It's easy to react with frustration or anger. However, staying calm and patient demonstrates emotional regulation and resilience. Take deep breaths, acknowledge your feelings, and communicate calmly. This teaches your child healthy coping mechanisms for handling stressful situations.

- **Effective Communication**

Open and honest communication fosters trust and understanding. Actively listen to your child's feelings, validate their concerns, and express your thoughts clearly and respectfully. Model respectful communication even when disagreeing, showcasing the importance of healthy dialogue.

- **Problem-Solving Skills**

When faced with challenges, don't just offer solutions; involve your child in problem-solving. Discuss options, consider consequences, and work together to find solutions. This equips them with the skills to tackle future challenges independently.

- **Organizational Skills**

Staying organized reduces stress and promotes productivity—model organizational skills by planning your day, keeping shared spaces tidy, and completing tasks efficiently. Encourage your child to participate in age-appropriate chores and help them develop routines for managing their belongings and responsibilities.

- **Emotional Regulation**

When you experience strong emotions, acknowledge them honestly. Share healthy coping mechanisms, like taking deep breaths, talking to a friend, or engaging in calming activities. This helps your child understand and regulate their own emotions in a healthy manner.

Chapter Takeaway

Operant conditioning is a learning process where behaviors are modified by their consequences. It's like a feedback loop: if a behavior leads to a positive outcome, it's more likely to be repeated; if it leads to a negative outcome, it's less likely to happen again.

Predictability reduces cognitive load and anxiety, allowing your child to direct his energy toward completing tasks rather than being unsure of what to do.

When your child constantly reacts to situations or scrambles to meet expectations, their confidence erodes, and they may feel easily frustrated. Taking proactive steps helps you build open communication and trust with your child.

Be a lifelong learner and role model positive personal growth. Be open to correction, and don't hesitate to apologize when you are wrong. It may not be easy at times, but I assure you, it is all for good.

We have laid the foundation for understanding the principles that drive learning and success. You have also seen the power of operant conditioning, where positive reinforcement encourages desired behaviors and the importance of predictability in reducing anxiety and fostering confidence. I also emphasized the role of proactive communication and positive role modeling in building trust and a growth mindset.

It's time to move beyond understanding and get into the practical. This next chapter will equip you with actionable techniques to unlock your child's potential.

5

HOW TO UNLOCK POTENTIAL BY USING EFFECTIVE TECHNIQUES FOR SCHOOL SUCCESS

"I am always ready to learn although I do not always like being taught."

– Winston Churchill

A recent study published in the Journal of Educational Psychology found that 72% of students have one challenge or another that prevents them from reaching their full potential academically. Knowing your child can do much better, yet watching them do so little can leave you helpless and unsure where to turn. This chapter will give you a lot of practical strategies to tackle the most common roadblocks and unlock your child's true potential.

Case Study

Amir stumbled through his first two years of elementary school. While his classmates were learning their numbers and alphabets, Amir seemed to exist in a fog. He kept flunking school tests, and his teachers were unsure if he understood anything being taught in school. Over time, he became less confident, and it seemed like he lost his shine. We spoke to teachers, who, while concerned, couldn't offer us the help we needed.

Doctors offered inconclusive diagnosis, leaving us adrift in a sea of uncertainty.

Then, a breakthrough came when we spoke to an educational psychologist. After a series of assessments, she told us Amir had ADHD. That was a relief because we finally knew what we were dealing with. We enrolled Amir in a program for ADHD kids. We also established a strong partnership with his school and tried to monitor his progress closely both at home and also at school.

The transformation was gradual but undeniable. Amir's eyes regained their sparkle as we took a different approach to his learning. He is still a little behind, but now, he can recite the whole alphabet without getting distracted, which is a big win for me.

I'm looking forward to more of it.

Recognizing and Addressing Academic Challenges

School is a big deal, no doubt, but coupled with ADHD, it is a much bigger deal. One of the reasons school might be an issue is difficulty with transitions. The school setting often involves a series of ever-changing actions and tasks. For kids with ADHD, this might be a little overwhelming. A child with difficulty transitioning might linger at an activity even when it's over, have difficulty switching gears between subjects, have frustration during schedule changes, and have emotional outbursts during transitions.

Difficulty with Transitions

You can address this by working with teachers to provide clear and concise warnings before transitions with visuals like countdown timers or pictures. Involve them by letting them choose a song to play while packing up or deciding which task to tackle first after the transition.

Break down transitions into smaller, more manageable steps. For example, instead of jumping straight from recess to math class, create an intermediary step like taking a short walk or organizing notebooks. Movement can also really help in refocusing. Integrate quick movement breaks into transitions, like jumping jacks or stretching exercises, to help them transition smoothly and refocus their energy.

Some boys benefit from sensory tools during transitions, like fidget toys or noise-canceling headphones; this helps them manage overwhelming stimuli and maintain focus.

Struggling to Follow Instructions

Another major academic challenge is struggling to follow instructions. This is usually characterized by incomplete tasks, asking for repeated instructions, misinterpreting directions, and frustration when presented with multi-step procedures. To help, you can use visual aids like pictures, diagrams, or written checklists to solidify their understanding. Repetition is important, so rephrase instructions differently and repeat key points for emphasis.

Instead of relaying a series of information, get them actively involved in understanding the instructions. Ask them to repeat the instructions or demonstrate their understanding through a simple task.

- **Social Rejection**

Your boy may also suffer from social rejection. To recognize this, look for signs of loneliness, isolation, difficulty making friends, withdrawal from social activities, or negative self-talk about social interactions. I discussed role-playing earlier; you can apply the same methods here again. Role-playing different social scenarios can help them develop coping mechanisms and practice positive communication strategies.

Encourage him to participate in activities he loves, like sports, music, or even dancing. Building confidence in their strengths can translate into better social interactions and a stronger sense of belonging. Help them establish positive connections with peers with similar interests or compatible personalities. This would encourage group activities and facilitate opportunities for collaboration.

- **Disruptiveness**

You also get to deal with disruptiveness. To help them refocus and avoid disruptive behavior, provide healthy outlets for their energy, such as fidget toys, movement breaks, or opportunities to help the teacher with small tasks. There is also a place for establishing predictable consequences for disruptive behavior, focusing on redirection rather than punishment. Time-outs, loss of privileges, or written reflections can help correct unwanted behavior.

Work with teachers and school counselors to develop an individualized behavior plan that outlines specific strategies for managing disruptive behavior in the classroom.

- **Reading Skill Stagnation**

If you notice slow reading speed, difficulty decoding words, poor comprehension, lack of interest in reading, and avoidance of reading tasks, your child may be dealing with reading skill stagnation. To address this, find books and reading materials that cater to their interests, like graphic novels, sports magazines, or high-interest non-fiction books. Audiobooks can also be a great way to keep them engaged while practicing comprehension skills.

Integrate activities that engage different senses alongside reading. Acting out scenes from the book or drawing illustrations can enhance his understanding and solidify his memory.

Setting Up Your Child For School Success

Nurturing a Positive Attitude Toward Learning

One way to set your child up for success at school is to nurture a positive attitude toward learning. You can do that by sparking your child's curiosity. Learn what his natural interests and passions are. Let him choose books on exciting topics, explore educational apps related to his hobbies, and engage in hands-on learning activities that fuel his enthusiasm.

You can also shift the focus from grades to the learning journey itself. Acknowledge their hard work, perseverance, and progress regardless of the final outcome. Highlight their strengths and encourage participation in activities where they excel. As stated earlier, positive reinforcement boosts their self-esteem and makes them feel capable in the classroom.

Find a Behavior Plan that Works

You also need to find a behavior plan that works. This will help you understand the underlying causes and functions of the presenting behavior, including the effects of trauma. You can equip yourself with the necessary skills and strategies to address or prevent such behaviors. It also clearly defines the situations in which any restricted practices can be used within the context of behavior management.

Involve your child, teachers, and applicable specialists in building a personalized behavior plan. This ensures consistency and tailored support across different environments.

Special Education Services and Accommodations

Some kids might need special education services and accommodations. You can have a professional evaluation to confirm if your child needs special education. This will help determine eligibility for special education services and Individualized Education Programs (more of that to come later). If your child requires an IEP, familiarize yourself with the accommodations outlined in the IEP, such as extended time for test-taking, preferential seating, or access to fidget toys.

I understand that it may not be so easy for you to send your child off to special education while you watch other kids thriving in the "normal" school system. It's part of the grief that comes with dealing with ADHD. What matters the most is ensuring that your child gets as much help as he needs, and if an IEP would provide that, why not go for it?

What Teachers Can do to Help

Teachers can provide a clear and consistent classroom routine with visual cues and reminders. They can also minimize distractions and maintain a predictable schedule to reduce anxiety and support focus. Teaching methods may also need to be adapted to cater to diverse learning needs. This might include using multisensory activities, graphic organizers, and technology tools.

Tips for Managing ADHD Symptoms at School

To manage ADHD symptoms at school, teach your child essential time management skills and give them age-appropriate organizers and planners to structure their workload. Breaking down tasks into smaller steps can make them feel more manageable. Also, encourage your child to communicate their needs to their teachers and peers.

Structured Routine

Before I go on, I would like to encourage you. It's okay to grieve the quiet mornings and predictable evenings you used to have. Your struggles do not reflect your parenting abilities; rather, your presence provides stability and guidance in a world that can feel overwhelming for your child. Celebrate the routines you've built, the battles you've won, and the moments of connection you've shared.

Every peaceful moment, work accomplished, and sincere smile is a win to be treasured. These are the milestones that mark your journey and prove the effectiveness of your efforts. This is a marathon, not a sprint. There will be disappointments and times when you feel frustrated, but perseverance will get you through the rough patches and support your child's growth. So, take a deep breath, and let's get right back into how to build a structured routine for your child.

Consistent Schedule

Consistency is the foundation of a good routine, and it extends beyond the weekdays to the weekends. This constant approach makes the child feel safer, reduces anxiety, and encourages a more balanced daily experience. As a result, keeping a consistent routine throughout the week is extremely important for creating continuity for the child.

Timer System

Integrating a timer system into the routine improves time management, which can be difficult for children with ADHD. These timers can be set for several activities, including homework or fun, and are effective for signaling task transitions. This organized use of time reduces resistance to change, allowing for a smoother transition between tasks.

Include Breaks and Movement

Breaks are also much needed to manage the energy levels of children with ADHD. Regular breaks, particularly during jobs requiring continuous concentration, might reduce restlessness and improve focus. Physical activities, such as short exercises or stretching, can also help them to release surplus energy and increase attention.

Homework Routine

So, how do you deal with homework? You can start offsetting a particular time each day for schoolwork. This creates a constant expectation and helps you work your schedule so you are available at that particular time every day. Creating a separate and well-organized homework space reduces distractions, allowing your child to be more focused, less distracted, and more attentive.

Daily Review

You can do a brief evaluation of your achievements and challenges at the end of each day. This reflective technique helps you keep a track record of your son's progress. Preferably, you can keep a journal. It might be hard at first, but as you keep at it, you are likely to get a little addicted to journaling. Don't say I didn't warn you. While it is good to have a structure, unexpected events may occur, so ensure you make room for needed changes.

Active Learning Techniques

Who says learning has to be stereotypic? Active learning techniques are a shift from traditional passive learning methods, encouraging students to actively engage in the learning process. In contrast to passive reception of information, active learning involves students in activities that stimulate critical thinking, problem-solving, and meaningful participation.

To facilitate active learning, you can create designated learning areas within your home using different tactile materials, scents, and textures. These stations are interactive environments where your child may explore and learn via touch, scent, and sound. You can use textured fabrics, scented items, and audio signals to make these stations more entertaining and informative.

Role-Playing

Did you know you can use drama to teach your child? You can use puppets, act out historical figures, or even encourage your child to create their own dramatic retellings of lessons. This approach builds a love for learning and helps retain information through creative expression.

You can also connect academic concepts to real-life situations by involving your child in practical scenarios. For instance, you can teach him to create a budget from behavioral charts and tokens. You both can create a list of his wants and cravings and set up a budget based on his points and tokens. This application of knowledge helps understanding and problem-solving skills.

Hands-On Activities

Encourage hands-on skills. You can give him simple building projects, art activities, or easy science experiments that can be done with household items. This creates a tangible and enjoyable way for your child to interact with educational concepts.

Dedicate a specific time for your child to delve into their personal interests and passions at home. This could involve building or any activity that genuinely captivates his curiosity. Leave him to express himself and enjoy himself while at it.

Utilize Technology

You can also make use of educational apps or games. These tools can make learning more dynamic and interactive, giving your child a unique perspective on various subjects. Ensure you supervise their screen time to balance educational engagement and other activities.

Ways To Help Your Child with Homework

I don't particularly like math; I guess my son picked that because he is usually edgy and fidgets even more whenever I try to help him with his math assignment. It took a while for me to figure out how to help without being a nuisance.

I also had to figure out his learning style. I discovered that my son prefers to read aloud rather than silently. He seems to get whatever is being taught when he reads the words back to himself. So, I allow him to read as many times as he wants while trying to offer explanations and pointers whenever he gets stuck.

Then, we usually go from known to unknown. I start with something he is very familiar with (sometimes, I revise the previous day's homework) before going into new or unfamiliar topics. After completing his task, I encourage him to reflect on what he has learned, what he really understands, and what he is yet to fully grasp. This helps me know where to pick up again next time.

We don't take in too much at a time. Quality effort in a focused period is more valuable than hours spent struggling without progress. So, I encourage him to take short breaks and return fresh.

Improve Overall Study Skills

Break down large tasks into smaller, manageable chunks with fixed time limits (e.g., 20 minutes per section). Use timers to signal breaks and transitions. Use mind maps, charts, and color-coding to organize information and improve visual memory.

You can also use memory aids like rhymes, acronyms, or songs to learn key concepts. Encourage activities like rewriting notes, summarizing aloud, or teaching the material to someone else. Teach him how to identify and tackle the most important tasks first.

Optimize Learning

Does your child learn best visually, audibly, or kinesthetically? Design study strategies that cater to their preferred style. Short breaks for physical activity (e.g., jumping jacks and stretches) can refocus attention and release pent-up energy.

I often start by ensuring that he understands core concepts before trying to solve questions. You can fill these knowledge gaps through online resources, tutoring, or revisiting previous lessons. Then, I also ensure that the environment is quite organized. We both don't do well in a clustered environment.

Increase Self Awareness

Discuss fidgeting, daydreaming, or feeling overwhelmed as signals to take a break or adjust their approach. Let him know it's okay to tell you when he needs rest or wants to take a short break. Encourage self-reflection on strengths, weaknesses, and preferred learning methods. Create a safe space for your child to discuss homework-related frustrations and challenges. Let him know, "It's okay to talk to Mum/Dad."

Maximize and Recognize Effort

Don't focus solely on the end goal. Acknowledge and celebrate their effort and progress, even if the final outcome isn't perfect. Help your son see the connection between effort and results. I repeatedly explained to my son that he would not be able to solve a math problem correctly if he didn't study and understand the formula.

Improve the Environment

Create a specific, well-organized space solely for homework, free from distractions and clutter. Ensure he has comfortable lighting and fresh air in the study space. Provide a comfortable chair and desk that promote good posture and minimize fatigue. You might need to turn off TVs, phones, and other electronic devices during homework time. Consider using website blockers or apps to manage online distractions. You can also use tools like audiobooks, text-to-speech software, or graphic organizers to aid his learning needs.

Educational Rights

Every child deserves access to a high-quality education tailored to their specific needs. Fortunately, two important federal laws in the United States protect this right: the Individuals with Disabilities Education Act (IDEA) and Section 504 of the Rehabilitation Act of 1973. These laws translate into two tools for students with disabilities: Individualized Education Programs (IEPs) and 504 Plans.

Individualized Education Program (IEP)

The Individualized Education Program (IEP) is specifically designed for students with disabilities outlined under IDEA, such as learning disabilities, intellectual disabilities, autism, deafness, blindness, and more. An IEP is a customized plan that outlines a student's specific needs, goals, and accommodations necessary to succeed in school. These can include tailored teaching methods and materials to address their learning style and challenges, additional support like speech therapy, occupational therapy, or counseling, and modifications to the curriculum or classroom environment, such as extended time for tests, preferential seating, or assistive technology. A team of professionals, including teachers, parents, specialists, and students, collaborate to create and implement the IEP.

504 Plan

The 504 Plan is for students with physical or mental impairments that substantially limit a major life activity but are not necessarily enough to qualify for an IEP. These are the ones who can benefit from a 504 Plan. This can include conditions like ADHD, dyslexia, anxiety, chronic illnesses, or allergies. A 504 Plan focuses on providing accommodations that ensure equal access to educational opportunities without changing the curriculum or lowering expectations. Examples include modifying assignments or tests, allowing alternative formats, providing additional breaks, or offering scribe support. There may be the need for classroom adjustments such as preferential seating, noise-canceling headphones, or access to fidget toys and ensuring teachers and school staff know the student's needs and implement the plan effectively.

While less formal than an IEP, a 504 Plan still requires collaboration between parents, teachers, and sometimes specialists. The plan outlines the specific accommodations needed and how they will be implemented.

Determining which plan is best depends on your child's unique needs and the support they require. You can speak with the school professionals to assess your child's strengths and challenges and advocate for the plan that provides the most effective support for their academic success.

Chapter Takeaway

- You can address difficulties in transitioning by working with teachers to provide clear and concise warnings before transitions with visuals like countdown timers or pictures. Involve them by letting them choose a song to play while packing up or deciding which task to tackle first after the transition.

- One way to prepare your child for success at school is to nurture a positive attitude toward learning, and you can do that by sparking your child's curiosity.

- This is a marathon, not a sprint. There will be disappointments and times when you feel frustrated, but perseverance will get you through the rough patches and support your child's growth.

Your child also has a life beyond the walls of the classroom. This next chapter will focus on another aspect of his life: social growth. School environments give rich opportunities for developing social skills like communication, teamwork, and empathy. Like transitions, your child will need some skills to have effective social interactions. In the next chapter, I will discuss these tools that will help your child build strong social connections.

6

BUILD BRIDGES, FOSTER SOCIAL GROWTH, AND HELP YOUR BOY THRIVE AMIDST PEERS

In a world that places a growing premium on social skills, education systems need to do much better at systematically fostering those skills across the school curriculum.

-Jose Angel Gurria

*S*trong friendships enrich our lives, and children with ADHD are no exception. Building relationships and making friends can feel like climbing Mount Everest for many children, but for those with ADHD, the climb can seem even more daunting. Seeing your beloved son struggle to connect with peers is not so easy. This chapter will help you break down social behaviors into manageable pieces and identify specific skills your child might struggle with, like starting conversations, taking turns, or reading social cues.

Case Study

Jerry liked being alone. He preferred playing games over talking to people who didn't understand him or, worse, might judge him. Talking in class was enough for him; Jerry didn't want to deal with his mom's new assignment about improving his social skills as if he didn't have enough to work on.

Connecting with others was hard for Jerry because he often acted without thinking and struggled to understand social cues. His parents wanted him to *join group activities and talk to people face-to-face. Even though Jerry didn't like the idea, his parents insisted it was important. They gave him a list of goals, like joining clubs and being more involved in conversations. Jerry was not so excited, but just maybe, he will give it a try.*

Breaking Down Social Behaviors

Identify Targeted Social Skills

Social interactions can sometimes be tricky for children, and they are even worse for kids with ADHD. But you can help them by simplifying social behaviors into manageable steps and guiding them on how to go about relating with others. Instead of addressing social skills as a whole, focus on specific areas for improvement. This can include greeting friends, sharing toys or taking turns. Observe your child in different situations to identify areas where they struggle or miss social cues.

Break Down Social Skills into Steps

Then, go ahead and break these behaviors into smaller steps. For example, you can show him that greeting a classmate involves making eye contact, smiling, saying "hello," and asking a friendly question. Use visual aids like charts or social scripts to represent these steps. Practice through role-playing in a safe environment, allowing your child to experiment and refine their skills. Praise him even with small successes to build confidence and encourage continued effort.

Provide Explicit Feedback

When offering feedback, be specific and constructive, focusing on what they can do differently next time. Use "I" statements to express observations and feelings, avoiding negative language. For instance, say, "I noticed you didn't make eye contact when you said goodbye. Can we do that again?"

Social Scripts

You can also offer scripts for common situations to prepare him to know how to act when faced with that situation in real time. Encourage personalization to make the scripts comfortable and unique. Gradually fade the scripts as your child becomes more confident, encouraging them to rely on their own social intuition.

Reinforce General Social Rules

Teach him the importance of empathy and respect for others' feelings and perspectives. Encourage active listening and genuine interest in what others have to say. Let him know that sometimes, listening rather than talking is okay. Help him recognize and interpret nonverbal cues like facial expressions, body language, and tone of voice.

How to Improve Social Skills in Children with ADHD

Determine the root cause of social ineptness

Before applying quick fixes, let's figure out the real issue. Is your child struggling with understanding social cues, impulsive blurting out, managing emotions, or finding it hard to take turns? Identifying the root cause allows you to tailor pacific strategies for skill development.

Assign your Child a Mission

Once you understand the challenge, you can make social interaction easier by introducing "missions." Assign your child a mission, such as introducing himself to someone new, complimenting him, or participating in a group activity.

Find Compatible Friends

You might also need to be on the lookout for the friends he keeps. Look for classmates who share their interests, understand their energy levels, and provide positive reinforcement. Encourage him to keep as many friends as he is comfortable, but remember, it's about quality over quantity. Even if it is just a single friend who gets him really well, encourage him to keep that friend.

Control the Activities and Environments

Opt for low-stimulus environments where they can focus and gradually build interactions. Start with small playdates or group activities with familiar faces, and slowly expand their social circle as they gain confidence. Teach him how to consider others' feelings and build genuine connections. Assure him that you will be there for and with him every step of the way. Your assurance is bound to boost his confidence.

Active Listening

Picture attempting to follow a whispered conversation in a crowded marketplace – that's the reality for many children with ADHD. Their minds constantly shift between sights, sounds, and thoughts, making sustained verbal communication a challenge. This frustration can lead to misunderstandings, missed instructions, and emotional outbursts.

Encourage Eye Contact

Eye contact is an important tool for focus. It helps ground the child in the present and also shows that he is interested in the conversation. Make eye contact and gently remind him to do the same when talking. Use playful prompts like "Show me your laser eyes."

Practice Patience

Avoid rushing. Give your child time to process what you're saying, filter out distractions, and formulate a response. Resist the urge to repeat yourself or bombard them with questions. Speak slowly and clearly, using simple sentences and avoiding technical jargon. It might be hard at first, but patience is a muscle that needs exercise, so please keep at it.

Ask Questions

Asking questions isn't just a way to gauge understanding; it's an invitation to engage. Instead of simply asking, "Did you hear what I said?" pose questions that require them to paraphrase or summarize the information. This helps them actively process the message and strengthens their memory. For instance, "Can you tell me what you remember about our plans for tomorrow?" or "What did you think about the story I just read?"

Empathy

Emotions tend to be amplified for children with ADHD. Joy can erupt into elation, while frustration can spiral into intense anger. This "blip-blip" effect makes it harder for them to regulate their emotions and respond calmly to situations. They may struggle to identify their feelings, leaving them confused and frustrated. This lack of recognition hinders their ability to deal with those emotions effectively.

Discuss Emotions

To help them cope:

1. Talk about his emotions.

2. Establish a safe space where your child can openly express their feelings, whether the joy of success or the sting of disappointment.

3. Use relatable scenarios, books, and movies to discuss characters'

emotions and motivations.

Understanding their own emotions is the first step towards understanding others'.

Encourage Perspective-Taking

The essence of perspective-taking is to help you step into someone else's shoes, feeling their joys and sorrows as if they were yours. Prompt your child to consider how the other person might feel and encourage them to think of ways to be kind rather than self-absorbed. ADHD usually brings intense emotions. Don't ignore or condemn their outbursts; instead, help them identify their triggers. Work with them to understand these triggers and how to find their way around it.

Model Empathetic Behavior

Children are adept mimics. Demonstrate what empathy looks like in action. Listen attentively to others, provide words of comfort and support, and genuinely celebrate their successes. When you make mistakes, admit them and show how to repair hurt feelings. While at it, train yourself to be an active listener. Your child is more likely to keep zoning out if he notices that you don't pay attention to him when he talks to you. Active listening is not limited to your son; you can translate this skill into other relationships. You will be a better person for it.

Set Up Social Goals

Assessment

Watch your child interact in various settings and discuss their social experiences openly. Ask questions like "What do you enjoy about playing with friends?" or "Are there times you feel uneasy in social situations?" Based on observations and discussions, pinpoint specific areas of difficulty. Are there challenges with initiating conversations, taking turns, or recognizing social cues?

Identify Specific Areas for Improvement

Spend time with your child and observe their social interactions. Do they struggle with taking turns, interrupting others, or recognizing emotional cues? Be specific about which behaviors you want to address. Talk to your child. Engage in open conversations about their social experiences. What do they find easy? What makes them feel uncomfortable?

To avoid overwhelming your child and allow for focused practice, target one or two specific areas at a time instead of broad improvements.

Make Goals Specific and Measurable

Ensure your goals are Specific, Measurable, Achievable, Relevant, and Time-bound. Instead of saying, "Be more social," opt for "Initiate a conversation with one new classmate at recess three times this week." Frame goals as positive actions instead of negatives. Instead of "stop interrupting," aim for "wait and raise your hand before speaking." Complex goals can feel overwhelming. Divide them into smaller, achievable steps with clear milestones.

Set clear and achievable goals using the SMART framework - Specific, Measurable, Attainable, Relevant, and Time-bound. For instance, "By the end of the month, I will greet one new classmate each day using eye contact and a friendly hello."

Involve Your Child

Involve your child in the goal-setting process. Discuss their needs and preferences, incorporating their input to enhance ownership and motivation. Divide each goal into smaller, manageable steps. For example, if the goal is to initiate conversations, start with practicing eye contact and saying "Hi!". Gradually introduce opportunities for real-life practice, beginning in low-pressure environments like playdates with familiar friends.

Create a Plan of Action

Work with your child to look for ways to achieve their goals. Role-playing social situations, using visual cues, or practicing social greetings can be helpful. Identify adults or peers who can offer support and encouragement. Enlist teachers or coaches to reinforce desired behaviors. You should also keep an open dialogue with your child and adjust the goals as needed.

Building and Nurturing Friendships

How ADHD Affects Friendships

Establishing and nurturing friendships is a journey that unfolds gradually, requiring a good dose of patience. This is because children with ADHD encounter several challenges in building and maintaining friendships. First, their impulsivity and emotional outbursts create difficulties controlling impulses, leading to misunderstandings and potentially fractured friendships. Additionally, attention difficulties make it hard for them to engage in conversations and potentially convey disinterest.

Challenges of ADHD and Friendships

Social cues are another issue they have to deal with. Recognizing them can be difficult at first, resulting in misinterpretations and awkward interactions. These challenges, in turn, can contribute to lower self-esteem, further complicating their ability to connect with others.

The initial steps, initiating conversations and sharing, can be particularly difficult, impeding the formation of those initial connections. Maintaining friendships introduces another layer of challenges, as following social rules proves demanding, leading to potential misunderstandings and conflicts.

How to Improve Friendships with ADHD

Help your child recognize their unique strengths and challenges. Open communication allows them to share their experiences and work through difficulties with friends. Practice active listening, taking turns, and asking questions. Role-playing scenarios can build confidence and teach appropriate responses. Follow through on commitments and respect plans. Use reminders and celebrate effort, even when unexpected challenges arise. Develop coping mechanisms like counting to ten or using fidget toys to avoid blurting or interrupting. Practice mindful responses before speaking. Encourage activities and groups aligned with your child's interests. Celebrate their individuality and help them connect with like-minded peers.

How Does Parental Involvement Help Kids with ADHD Make Friends?

Supporting kids with ADHD in making friends involves teaching them valuable social skills. Focus on their strengths and encourage open communication. Creating opportunities for socializing, like arranging playdates or getting involved in clubs or activities aligned with their interests, can also help their social experience.

How Can Parents Maintain Patience and Perspective?

Remember, it takes time. Building friendships takes effort and practice. Don't get discouraged by setbacks. Avoid comparing your child to others. Every child develops at their own pace, especially one with ADHD. Focus on his strengths and interests and learn to manage your own emotions. It's natural to feel worried or frustrated, you should take some time out for yourself. You need some "me" time. Taking some time off doesn't make you a bad Dad or Mom. It simply gives you the chance to unwind and refresh. Connecting with fellow parents of children with ADHD can also do a lot of good.

Chapter Takeaway

- Social interactions can sometimes be tricky for children; it gets even worse for kids with ADHD. But you can help them by simplifying social behaviors into manageable steps and guiding them on how to relate with others.

- Be on the lookout for the friends he keeps. Look for classmates who share their interests, understand their energy levels, and provide positive reinforcement. Encourage him to keep as many friends as he is comfortable, but remember, it's about quality over quantity. Even if it is just a single friend who gets him really well, encourage him to keep that friend.

- Avoid rushing. Give your child time to process what you're saying, filter out distractions, and formulate a response. Resist the urge to repeat yourself or bombard them with questions.

Social skills are just one piece of the puzzle. To thrive, your child will need to develop strong executive functioning skills. These encompass abilities like planning, organization, time management, and emotional regulation. This next chapter will show you all you need to know about executive functioning skills development. As you use these strategies in the next chapter, you can groom your child to become the confident, capable boy he is meant to be.

7

THE ROADMAP TO EXECUTIVE FUNCTIONING AND SKILLS DEVELOPMENT

"Executive function challenges are often mistaken for disobedience, laziness, defiance, or apathy."

–Chris Zeigler Dendy

*E*xecutive Function (EF) skills are the cognitive abilities that govern planning, organization, time management, and emotional regulation. Your boy will need these kids for success in various aspects of life, including academics, social interactions, and daily routines. Research has shown that 72% of children with ADHD exhibit at least one EF deficit. These deficits can manifest as difficulty prioritizing tasks, managing time, staying organized, and regulating emotions. Untreated EF issues can lead to academic struggles, social difficulties, and decreased self-esteem.

This chapter sheds more light on the different aspects of Executive functioning and highlights how each of these skills plays out in our everyday decisions and interactions. It also delves into a little bit of science behind these skills. It helps to understand what happens with executive functioning in an individual with ADHD while suggesting strategies to help navigate living with ADHD.

Case Study

Miles, my twelve-year-old son, had a knack for forgetting to turn in his math homework. It wasn't because he wasn't smart – the kid was sharp. His brain just didn't play nice when remembering things like handing in assignments. As his dad, watching the struggle was like sitting through a never-ending sitcom of mishaps. Each forgotten homework felt like a tiny dagger – not super painful, but annoying enough to make you cringe.

Miles's brain was a bit of a rebel, not following the usual rules. And as a Dad, seeing your kid wrestling with something as basic as turning in homework was tough. The potential was there, the brightness in his eyes, but he just couldn't get the most basic things done.

Executive Functioning and ADHD

Executive Functioning (EF) skills are cognitive abilities that enable humans to perform goal-oriented tasks. In simple terms, EF entails all mental and neural processes that enable an individual to set a goal, work toward achieving that goal, and adapt (or even leverage) constantly changing circumstances in our day-to-day lives as we pursue those goals. It also helps us maximize our relationships with friends, partners, teammates, and the rest of the world.

Areas of Executive Function

Let me branch into science a little bit. The mammalian brain can be divided into four lobes: the frontal, parietal, temporal, and occipital. Each is responsible for various functions. The occipital lobe is said to be responsible for vision. The temporal and parietal lobes are said to be concerned with short-term memory and spatial orientation, respectively, among a host of other functions. (John Hopkins) This leaves us with the frontal lobe. The frontal lobe involves movement, decision-making, speech ability, and personality.

The Prefrontal Cortex (PFC) covers the foremost part of the frontal lobe and is principally responsible for executive functioning in humans. It also connects with other regions of the brain to perform these functions.

Many psychologists have expanded the skills responsible for executive functioning in different ways. For the purpose of this chapter, working memory, inhibitory control, cognitive flexibility, and problem-solving will be discussed briefly.

Working Memory

Working memory is the ability to temporarily store a small amount of information and recall it quickly to process and understand other information.. Sounds chunky right?

Let's take an example. If I told you, 'Tommy eats breakfast next door. He then comes to mine for some juice.' You would need to first retain who the subject 'Tommy' is, what he does and where he does it, so you could understand the next statement. This is how working memory works. An individual has to be able to pick and retain important parts of a large piece of information, to make sense of the whole idea. Let's say you wanted to see Tommy but didn't know where he lived; you could just come to my house tomorrow morning after breakfast. This way, working memory enhances reasoning, decision-making, and planning, which we have to do in our daily lives.

Inhibitory Control

Did you ever feel like screaming your head off to someone who really acted like a pest around you, but you didn't? Instead, you faked a smile and stylishly excused yourself. Inhibitory Control is a skill that enables us to control our innate urges and ensures we do not do the first irrational thing that crosses our minds in a given situation.

There are four types of inhibitory control, namely, behavioral, emotional, cognitive, and motor inhibitory control (Hills Academy).

Behavior inhibitory control involves the ability to control the urge to behave badly, especially when we are around company. It serves to help us manage our social interactions.

Emotional inhibitory control helps us control our emotional responses to situations we encounter. It helps us to hold in the tantrums or keep from spontaneously bursting into tears because we can't find our favorite T-shirt. This skill is responsible for the emotional regulation function of the Prefrontal Cortex.

Cognitive Inhibitory Control keeps us focused on the task at hand despite many other things happening in the background. It helps us meet that deadline despite having our friends over as they share the hot gist on the new neighbor with the hot body.

Motor inhibitory control keeps us grounded and enables us to remain seated or standing even when we are nervous as the new boss invites us to chat in his office or when we are excited about getting our orders filled at the new restaurant without pulling everyone in front out of the line (even when the thought crosses our minds)

Cognitive Flexibility

This explains an individual's ability to be mentally flexible. This flexibility is evidenced by the ease of moving from thinking about one concept to another. The ability to adapt to unforeseen challenges and detours as one goes about daily tasks also shows a cognitive flexibility skill that is on par.

Problem-solving

Problem-solving is the ability to successfully identify, define, strategize, and follow through to overcome obstacles and achieve an intended goal. It refers to the ability to focus on the end goal as hurdles arise instead of getting blindsided and tangled up in the difficult situation at hand.

How ADHD Affects Executive Functioning Skills

Having learned about executive functioning and some of the ways it influences our lives, it becomes easier to identify how ADHD impacts Executive Functioning Skills. ADHD is a disorder which is caused by a difference in brain development. Remember the PFC? Research has shown that individuals with ADHD have an underactive/unregulated Prefrontal Cortex, which affects the ability of most people diagnosed with ADHD to carry out the functions explained above.

It is not uncommon to see a kid with ADHD struggle as he tries to recall a small amount of information that he has come in contact with on various occasions as compared to other kids in his age range. Once, I interacted with a parent who shared how her daughter would always ask for her friend's phone number every single morning, even though she had been calling her for more than a whole school term.

Executive Function Deficits Common in Kids with ADHD.

ADHD can be characterized predominantly by three main observations. They are impulsivity, hyperactivity, and attention difficulty. Although this doesn't mean every child with ADHD fits into all three molds at once- some present with just two- these three symptoms are usually tell-tale signs of ADHD.

Impulsivity can be related to a deficit in behavioral inhibitory control. This could translate into a child being unable to wait their turn, blurting out answers before they are finished due to excitement, or rushing through assignments without taking time to think answers through. Hyperactivity has been said to stem from a lack of motor inhibitory control as the child is restless, fidgets a lot, finds it hard to keep still or stand up, and runs around at inappropriate moments.

Attention difficulty suggests reduced cognitive flexibility, poor cognitive inhibitory control, and poor working memory. This makes it seem that the child is extremely forgetful, as switching between many thoughts becomes increasingly difficult, or the child cannot tune out external stimuli or other thoughts. Emotional dysregulation is also present in these kids. This could mean the child swings from one extreme of the emotional or mood spectrum to another.

Poor working memory could lead to poor long-term memory, making it difficult to do well on tests and assignments.

Common Misperceptions of Executive Function Among Parents

Many parents are unfamiliar with Executive Function (EF) and can make common misperceptions that may hinder their ability to support their children effectively. Here are some of the most common misconceptions:

1. Intelligence vs. Effort:

Misconception: "My child is smart, so why do they struggle with organization and focus?"

Reality: EF skills are independent of intelligence. A child can be highly intelligent but struggle with planning, time management, or emotional regulation due to underdeveloped EF skills.

2. Lazy vs. Unmotivated:

Misconception: "My child just needs to try harder; they're lazy."

Reality: Difficulty with EF can overwhelm tasks or lead to procrastination. It's not a lack of motivation but an inability to break down tasks, manage time effectively, or regulate emotions while working.

3. Willpower vs. Skill Deficit:

Misconception: "If they just focus and put in the effort, they can overcome these challenges."

Reality: EF skills are not just about willpower but about underlying cognitive processes. Just telling a child to focus won't address their underlying challenges.

4. Outgrowing vs. Ongoing Needs:

Misconception: "They'll eventually outgrow these issues."

Reality: While EF skills develop with age, some individuals with ADHD or other learning differences may continue to struggle with EF, even as adults. Ongoing support and strategies are crucial.

5. Medical vs. Behavioral Issue:

Misconception: "This must be a medical condition requiring medication."

Reality: While some medical conditions can impact EF, difficulties in this area can also be due to learning differences, environmental factors, or lack of skill development.

Effective Communication

Conversations are an integral part of our everyday lives. The majority of our lives are spent on receiving, processing, interpreting, and storing information. Once or twice a day, everyone has issues communicating with others effectively. However, this can get a little difficult when ADHD is thrown into the mix. Kids with ADHD sometimes struggle with paying attention to a speaker over an extended period of time, especially when there are a lot of external stimuli. They may blurt out words without even thinking about what they mean, and some might get distracted mid-sentence and completely forget the question or what they were talking about. You know, poor working memory and all that stuff. Let me share some coping strategies for effective communication in ADHD.

Maintain Clear and Simple Communication

As with everyone else, it is important that communication be as simple and clear as possible. For example, instead of saying, 'Get ready for bed,' one can say, 'Go to the bathroom and brush your teeth,' This is quite simple and cuts to the point.

The strategy works especially when giving instructions because the whole statement is a very small amount of information. Therefore, it is easier for working memory to pick and retain the main point, 'brush.'

It could also be used when talking to a child so they don't zone you out. One could break down different ideas into simpler statements and ask the child questions to ensure they are listening or can process the information before adding more.

- **Establish Eye Contact**

Eye contact is important for helping a child retain focus while communicating. It is extremely important to make eye contact with a child as opposed to just addressing him when his attention could be entirely on something or someone else in the background. When a child looks at a speaker who's giving instructions or sharing information, it becomes a little easier to follow and pick up non-verbal clues from the conversation.

- **Provide Structure and Predictability**

As a result of reduction in the ability to shift seamlessly from thinking on one concept to another in an individual with ADHD, it becomes necessary to bring structure and predictability into conversations. This enables the child to fully and completely process one thought before moving on to another, thus reducing confusion. It also mitigates distraction as understanding of one concept, opens the child up the more to receiving and understanding the next. This might not be the case when a conversation has no structure and rapidly moves from one concept to another, as the child becomes overwhelmed, tunes out of the conversation and finds something a little bit less cognitive easier to focus on.

- **Encourage Self-Expression**

Self expression aids effective communication by helping your child gather the myriad number of thoughts that cross his mind. Encouraging self expression as a parent, makes it easier for your child to identify and then sort appropriately his ideas or feelings so he can clearly share them with others. Common ways encourage self expression including encouraging a child to write down his thoughts as opposed to blurting them out, spending time listening to a child verbalize what he thinks without judgment by social standards.

Problem-Solving Skills

In children with ADHD, the combination of hyperactivity, impulsivity and inattention makes problem solving a not so easy process. However, processes to this skill can be taught, which over time, enables the children to apply them to solve problems in different situations no matter how simple or complex.

- **Use Concrete Examples**

Stephanie loved animations but totally dreaded doing her homework. Assignment times were often characterized by yelling, tantrums, tears and shouts. It just felt easier to watch Frozen and spend the whole evening singing 'Let it go'. But her school work was suffering and she needed to do better.

One evening, her mum sat with her on the couch and said gently, 'Steph,your school work is suffering and you need to do your assignments better. What do you think we can do to make it easier?

Stephanie says what if she didn't do homework at all. Her mum calmly let her know it was going to affect her grades. She suggests that Stephanie gets extra fifteen minutes to watch her favorite animation if she focuses really hard on her homework and doesn't throw tantrums. Stephanie suggests Mummy plays Anna and she plays Elsa whenever they do homework. A compromise is reached. The next time homework gets done, Stephanie is a bit more pliant.

- **Define the Problem**

The first step in problem solving is to identify and define the problem in clear terms. It is important that this be done as calmly and reassuringly as possible, because yelling could close the child off to assessing the situation objectively. It should go straight to the point and make use of concrete examples that the child can relate to.

- **Brainstorming**

The next step is to encourage the child to suggest ways he thinks the problem can be solved. In the example above, Stephanie's mom asked her what she thought they could do about homework time. Listen actively to your child as she shares ideas on solving the problem. Share some of your own to help the child's think of more ideas. It is important that the process is not rushed.

- **Evaluate and Choose**

This step takes into consideration the fact that not all of the ideas you have brainstormed will be useful or feasible. Calmly examine each option with your child, pointing out areas you think would make it not the best option at the moment. One must ensure that the child is not made to feel they can't think properly as ideas are jettisoned. Discard the ideas, not the child's feelings.

After evaluation, options that seem feasible should be agreed and acted upon. It is always a good idea to incorporate a reward system as an incentive for problem solving. In Stephanie's case, she gets extra TV time.

- **Encourage Flexibility**

As these ideas are implemented, it is necessary for you and your child to assess whether or not they are working to improve the situation or not. If they are, it is best to keep at it and once again, look for ways to improve upon them and switch things up. If not, feel free to stop working with them and begin the brainstorming process again. It is however extremely important that your child agrees that it is not serving to improve the situation of the problem at hand, he or she could even explain why they think it's not working. This is advantageous on so many levels, i that it helps your child learn the importance of reassessment in problem solving, makes them comfortable with exploring options as well as actually solving the problem at hand.

Organizational Skills

Kids with ADHD are sometimes labeled as disorganized people who have trouble meeting deadlines, are constantly losing school supplies, forgetting important stuff to bring along and have very disorganized desks or lockers.

While it is fairly normal for all children at a certain age group to occasionally lose things or forget stuff, poor working memory in children with ADHD makes these phenomena more often than not and causes interference with daily life. The impairment of this EF skill causes pre-planning and follow through inability in kids, which in turn leads to disorganization. What are coping techniques for deficit in organizational skills

- **Visual Aids and Tools**

Getting activities, deadlines and required materials as physical as they can get, can boost a child's working memory. The use of a color coded filing system helps the child get all the necessary supplies for his classes. How this works is, different notes, textbooks and other books related to a subject can be wrapped in a red book cover, the next subject in a green one and so on.

The child over time knows, red is for science, green is for math and blue is for arts. This helps his chances that he takes everything he needs along, as he moves from one class to the next.

Apart from color codes, labeling containers, baskets and folders come in handy. Cloth bins could be labeled 'socks', 'beanie', 'pants' or 'dirty'. Separate folders for completed or undone assignments could be created. The act of attaching labels to storage helps the child's brain easily recognize where to keep what and where to find what, thereby encouraging organization.

Another visual tool that can help your child stay organized is the use of calendars for tracking activities. Writing out future appointments or deadlines and pasting them where your child can see them prevents the mad rush that accompanies forgotten deadlines.

- **Establish Routines**

Routines are an excellent way to enhance organization in kids with ADHD. Because of the inability to anticipate and quickly switch between changing cognitive patterns, routine helps the ADHD brain get more familiar and forethink his action in the given situation. For example, a checklist time could be adopted before and after school time, homework could be done after siesta when your child is well rested and a little bit more refreshed, or just before video game time which could be a reward. Clean up time could be scheduled for early Saturday morning. With constant practice, routines afford your child the opportunity to anticipate and plan out specific actions for familiar circumstances.

- **Set Clear Expectations**

Setting clear expectations for what organization means or looks like can help the child achieve it. Instead of getting ready for school, one could tell the child to pack his bag, take his bath, wear his clothes, get his lunch and head out for school. Organizing your room can be translated into, pick all toys into the closet, all dirty clothes into the laundry bin etc. This helps the child focus more on performing the actions instead of getting sidetracked trying to figure out what to do.

- **Use Checklists**

Let's say you are hosting a group of co-workers for your night out in your home and you have decided to treat them to a plate of your grandma's award-winning dish. Recipe settled, you head to the nearest grocery store to pick up the ingredients. Moments later you return to your chicken and are halfway through the recipe before you realized you had forgotten one main ingredient. You have no choice. You must return to the store or risk shaming your beloved Granny's memory. If only you had made a list.

Checklists are life savers as they reduce the risk of forgetting important materials needed for the day. Before and after school checklists can be incorporated into our child's routine. These checklists could make use of questions such as 'Have all textbooks been packed?' 'Are gym clothes in the bag?' 'Any homework due?' and so on. Checklists serve to enhance readiness for the day's task.

- **Teach Prioritization**

The inability to properly anticipate, plan and follow through action plans play a major role in the disorganization exhibited in ADHD kids. When there are clear action plans, poor cognitive inhibitory control, kids with ADHD tend to skim through actions or tasks which require high level cognition in favor of those that don't. So a boy might decide to play video games instead of doing arithmetic. Then when it's time to turn in his homework, quickly writes the first answer and makes 'careless' mistakes which they shouldn't have made.

In order to reduce the incidence of this, kids must be taught to prioritize important tasks over the less important ones. This might require a broad explanation about the long term benefits of a specific action in a way the child can understand, incorporating reward for priority actions, encouraging self expression. Self expression is a way to enable the child to voice out reasons for wanting to procrastinate. This can give a parent pointers on how to help them break out of fear and tackle important and urgent tasks.

Time Management

ADHD kids have a very poor sense of timing. Sense of timing is the ability to accurately (or near accurately) predict the amount of time that has passed without actually checking the time. Between dealing with this impairment in function and the consequences of disorganization as well as high level forgetfulness, individuals with ADHD are often late for appointments, deadlines or completely miss them altogether.

- **Use Visual Timers**

To help children with ADHD manage their time effectively, it is important to teach them how to use Visual Timers. Visual timers help to make time more physical to them. Remember that executive functioning skills are highly cognitive (mental, can't be seen per say), so utilizing physics ways to deal with these mental things go a long way in ensuring effective learning. As children go about their tasks, using timers set at specific periods (10 minutes, 15minutes) can help them know how much time has gone so they can keep up focus or jog them to reality when attention wanders.

- **Create a Visual Schedule.**

This helps your child effectively spend time on important things that really need attention. By creating a to-do list for after school, you help your child focus his energy on performing duties that actually count for a peaceful week or school day. In creating a schedule, it is imperative that your child gets to contribute in the planning. Let the schedule contain activities that your child genuinely loves to do.

- **Use External Reminders.**

What good is a to-do list which one forgets to check or actually does. External reminders such as alarms help to consolidate the effectiveness of to-do lists in your child's everyday life. Alarms can be set for each activity already mapped out in the to-do list.

Combining these three strategies will go a long way in improving your child's sense of timing.

Emotional Regulation

Having learnt a little about how the Prefrontal Cortex influences the exhibition of executive functioning skills in humans, it becomes necessary to talk about another important brain structure known as the amygdala. Situated below the junction of the brain hemispheres, the amygdala is the part of the brain responsible for attaching emotions to experiences.

In a typical brain, the amygdala is highly regulated. However in ADHD, it is said to be overactive. What this means for people with ADHD is that they seem unable to control emotional response or react appropriately in certain circumstances. They can experience sharp mood swings in a short period of time. Tantrums or bursts of anger are also common traits. There is also a marked difficulty in returning to a calm state after excitement.

- **Emotion Identification**

In order to aid emotional regulation in kids with ADHD, parents should teach and encourage their wards to identify and label specific ways they are feeling at any point in time. A child who is upset because he has no one to play with at recess should be taught to express his sadness. Children should be given the opportunity to identify and define emotions of joy, anger, sadness, worry and the likes. This provides the adult with an opening to help the child get calm.

- **Modeling**

As a parent, modeling calmness in the face of provocation or excitement is key as it helps your child learn appropriate ways to react in certain situations. Especially when your child is currently in a bout of uncontrolled emotional response, keeping calm becomes very instrumental in helping your child return to rest.

Instead of yelling or calling out threats as the child throws tantrums, concentrate on maintaining peace and quiet in your core. Calmly invite the child to talk about it when he/she is ready.

Mindfulness and Relaxation Techniques such as deep breathing and meditation provide a means of helping the child calm down after an emotional high. Sometimes, they can even come in as the first line of action in order to apply other strategies such as emotional identification.

- **Combination Therapy**

As everyday continues the quest to improve executive functioning skills in children with ADHD, it is essential to adopt strategies that work based on the personalized needs of one's child. Exploring other alternatives such as medication, cognitive behavioral therapy (CBT), neurofeedback (a type of brain training that relies on the neuroplasticity of the brain- new brain cells can be retrained to pick up certain function) and exercise (increases production of endorphins -happy hormones- such as dopamine, serotonin and epinephrine which helps emotion regulation and focus) can provide a well-rounded skills needed for your child to live his life to its maximum capacity.

Chapter Takeaway

- In simple terms, EF entails all mental and neural processes that enable an individual to set a goal, work towards achieving that goal, adapt (or even leverage) constantly changing circumstances that happen in our day-to-day lives as we pursue those goals.

- As with everyone else, it is important that communication be as simple and clear as possible. For example, instead of saying, 'go get ready for bed', one can say, 'go to the bathroom and brush your teeth'. Quite simple and cuts to the point.

- The first step in problem solving is to identify and define the problem in clear terms. It is important that this be done as calmly and reassuringly as possible, because yelling could close the child off to assessing the situation objectively. It should go straight to the point and make use of concrete examples that the child can relate to.

- A child who is upset because he has no one to play with at recess should be taught to express his sadness. Children should be given the opportunity to identify and define emotions of joy, anger, sadness, worry and the likes. This provides the adult with an opening to help the child get calm.

Even with strong EF skills, everyday living may not go as planned, and for children with ADHD, these bumps can sometimes trigger intense emotional responses known as meltdowns. These moments can be overwhelming for both the child and those around them. This next chapter focuses on navigating meltdowns, you will learn how to recognize the warning signs of a brewing meltdown and also create a safe and supportive environment to help your child weather the storm.

.

8

NAVIGATE THE STORM: STRATEGIES FOR HANDLING ADHD MELTDOWNS AND TOUGH DAYS

"Tantrums are not bad behavior. Tantrums are an expression of emotion that becomes too much for the child to bear. No punishment is required. What your child needs is compassion and safe, loving arms to unload in."

—— *Rebecca Eanes*

*M*eltdowns are almost inevitable when dealing with ADHD. These intense emotional episodes can be overwhelming and disruptive, impacting not only the kids but also those around them. This chapter will help you understand the whys and hows of the ADHD meltdowns. I'll show you tips and tricks on how to manage them drawing on both current research and my personal experiences.

Case Study

Festus wiped the sweat from his brow, he was exhausted. The sun dipped below the horizon, casting long shadows across the small living room. His son, Justin, sat on the threadbare couch, his face contorted in frustration.

"Enough, Justin!" Festus's voice cracked. "Why can't you just behave like other kids?"

Justin's tantrums were relentless. Festus had tried everything—counting to ten, deep breaths, even seeking advice from well-meaning friends. But Justin's outbursts just wouldn't let up. Festus worked two jobs to keep food on the table and a roof over their heads. The factory during the day, the janitorial shift at night. He'd come home bone-tired, only to find Justin's toys scattered across the floor.

His wife, Irene, had left them years ago. "I can't handle it," she'd said, tears streaming down her face. "I need peace." Festus understood, but he couldn't abandon his son. Justin was his flesh and blood. But at this rate, he just wasn't sure of how much more he could take in.

Tantrums and ADHD

Tantrums are a common part of early childhood development, typically between 1 and 5 years old. It's children's way of children learning to communicate their needs and manage their emotions. Although these tantrums can be quite annoying to parents, they help kids express frustration, fatigue, or feeling overwhelmed.

- **How Tantrums are a Sign of ADHD**

Tantrums alone are not diagnostic of ADHD. Many children without ADHD experience tantrums. However, children with ADHD are more likely to experience more frequent, intense, and longer-lasting tantrums compared to their peers. Different areas of your child's brain can manage things like focusing, controlling feelings, and processing information. In ADHD, some of these areas might have swings that go a little too high or slides that are a bit too fast.

- **Symptoms That Can Influence Tantrums**

Sensory overload: Bright lights, loud noises, or even itchy clothes can irk your child, making them irritable and prone to meltdowns.

Trouble with emotions: Understanding and managing feelings can be tough. Frustration, disappointment, or even excitement can quickly escalate into tantrums if your child doesn't know how to express them effectively.

Impulsivity: Acting before thinking is common in ADHD. This can lead to saying or doing things they regret, triggering a tantrum in response to the consequences.

Difficulties with attention: Staying focused can also be a problem. When they lose track of instructions or forget what they are doing, it can lead to confusion and frustration, sometimes expressed through tantrums.

- **Differences Between Typical and ADHD-Related Tantrums**

While specific desires or frustrations might trigger typical tantrums, ADHD-related tantrums can look a bit different:

Intensity and Duration: You can picture a regular tantrum like a pot on the stove simmering. An ADHD-related tantrum is like a pot boiling over, with intense emotions and longer outbursts that are harder to calm down from.

Triggers: Typical tantrums often have clear triggers, like wanting a toy. ADHD-related tantrums might seem to appear "out of nowhere," triggered by something seemingly insignificant or even internal, like sensory overload.

Emotional Regulation: Calming down after a typical tantrum usually happens with some reassurance and patience. For children with ADHD, managing emotions during and after a tantrum can be much more challenging.

Why Do Tantrums Occur

You will most likely get a lot of tantrums, I got a heap load of mine also. Knowing why these tantrums occur will help you know how to deal with them. Your kid may throw a tantrum for a number of reasons. This includes (but definitely not limited to):

- **Persistent Irritability**

This can stem from several factors in ADHD, including difficulties processing information. Children with ADHD find it difficult to understand instructions, organize thoughts, and follow expectations. This can lead to confusion and frustration, manifesting as irritability. As I said earlier, managing emotions effectively can be hard for children with ADHD. They might struggle to understand or express their feelings, leading to frustration and irritability.

- **Increased Impatience, Particularly When Stressed**

Waiting, transitions, and even unexpected changes can be significant stressors for children with ADHD. Their internal "patience meter" runs down pretty quick, leading to meltdowns when it runs out. Imagine having a timer constantly ticking down, knowing things might go wrong when it hits zero. This is the pressure some children with ADHD feel.

- **Overreactions in Response to Minor Stressors:**

What seems like a small issue to you might feel like the whole world to your child. This is because distractions are easily picked up, making it hard to ignore minor stressors. It's like having a spotlight constantly scanning the environment, highlighting every potential inconvenience. Finding solutions to challenges can be trickier for children with ADHD. This frustration can build and manifest as an overreaction when faced with even minor stress.

- **Intense Emotions**

This is a big blessing but can sometimes feel like a curse. Children with ADHD experience joy, excitement, and love with great intensity. But the flip side is that negative emotions like anger, frustration, and sadness can feel overwhelming and difficult to manage. Imagine driving a food truck with no brakes - that's how their emotions sometimes feel.

- **Outbursts of Explosive Anger**

When intense emotions reach a peak, they might erupt in an outburst of anger. This isn't intentional "bad behavior" but rather a struggle to manage the overwhelming emotions. Think of a pressure cooker - if the valve doesn't release safely, the built-up pressure will eventually explode.

- **Difficulty Expressing Anger in Words**

Putting feelings into words can be challenging for anyone, but even more so for children with ADHD. They might struggle to identify and articulate their emotions, leading to meltdowns as their only way to express themselves. Imagine being stuck in a super cold room with no way to communicate your discomfort - that's how they might feel when unable to express their anger verbally.

Behavioral Problems Associated with ADHD

- **Rage and Temper Tantrums**

I had a pressure cooker I used for years, but even when it broke, I held onto it, unable to let go. Now, imagine that pressure cooker simmering on the stove, but instead of food, it's filled with intense emotions, frustrations, and sensory overload. For children with ADHD, difficulty regulating these internal experiences can feel like pressure building and building until it explodes in an outburst we might perceive as rage. It's not intentional anger but an overwhelming release they struggle to control.

- **Will not listen to people in authority**

You might also notice that your child would just not listen to people in authority. This isn't always intentional defiance. Children with ADHD may struggle with auditory processing, making it hard to register and understand instructions fully. Additionally, impulsivity and difficulty focusing can make it challenging to consistently follow through on requests, creating the impression of disobedience. Imagine trying to listen to someone in a crowded room with constant distractions – that's how hearing instructions can feel for them.

- **Getting Annoyed Easily and Intentionally annoys others**

Remember the pressure cooker analogy? Small things that wouldn't bother most children can feel like poking that simmering pot for children with ADHD. Their heightened sensitivity to sights, sounds, and sensory input can trigger frustration and annoyance more easily. While frustrating, intentionally annoying others, rarely stems from malice. Children with ADHD often crave attention and struggle with social cues, leading to actions that unintentionally annoy others. It might be a misguided attempt to connect, a cry for attention, or simply a result of not understanding social norms as readily.

- **Blaming others**

Another behavioral problem common to ADHD kids is the unwillingness to take responsibility for their actions. In moments of frustration or confusion, they might blame others for situations they contributed to, not out of malice, but because it's easier to process than accepting responsibility when feeling emotionally overloaded.

How to Handle Tantrums

While speaking to kids, I often ask them, "If you could magically change one thing, anything at all, what would it be?" The usual answers are escaping school, having a super long recess, snagging a pet like a dog or a pony, going on a moon trip, or having an endless supply of ice cream.

Now, kids dealing with ADHD have a similar wish, but it's not about daily treats. Most of them just want their behavior to be magically better and to be able to pay attention more. They also wish their parents wouldn't get so upset with them. When I hear this from so many ADHD kids, it hits me how badly they don't want to be seen as 'bad.' They're asking for help with stuff that's tough to control.

Here's the deal: Your kid isn't trying to be stubborn, unruly, or lazy. ADHD isn't just a behavior thing; it's a medical deal tied to how the brain works, influenced by genes, diet, and surroundings, not just bad behavior.

So, bottom line: Your kid's not a 'bad' kid, and you're not a 'bad' parent. No one's to blame for ADHD. Blaming yourself or others and trying to fix things with criticism won't help. Tantrums aren't about being "bad" but symptoms of the underlying challenges associated with ADHD. Here are some strategies to help you through these moments:

- **Showing the Child How to Behave**

Instead of focusing on what not to do during a tantrum, fill their toolbox with skills for calming down. Teach them deep breathing exercises, counting techniques, or positive self-talk phrases they can use when feeling overwhelmed. Practice these skills together when things are calm. Role-play different scenarios so your child feels prepared to use these tools when a tantrum starts.

- **Repeating the Rules**

This might be a little dicey. Setting clear expectations is important, but repeating the same rule repeatedly during a tantrum can fuel the fire. Your child might already feel frustrated and confused, and repeatedly hearing the same thing can make them shut down.

Instead, try relating with the cause of concern and offer to hear them out. For example, you could say, "I understand you're upset, but throwing toys hurts others. Why not tell me how you feel in as much detail as possible." Focus on positive reinforcement when your child follows the rules. Praise them for taking turns, using their words nicely, or calming down when frustrated.

- **Taking Care of Their Needs**

Often, tantrums are triggered by something deeper than a broken toy or missed snack. Your child might be hungry, tired, overwhelmed by sensory input, or struggling to communicate their needs. Take a moment to check in with your child's basic needs. Offer them a snack, a quiet space to relax, or help them express their feelings in words. Addressing these underlying needs can prevent future tantrums and help your child learn to regulate their emotions more effectively.

- **Distracting the Child**

Sometimes, shifting your child's attention can help de-escalate a tantrum before it escalates further. This can be especially helpful for younger children or when the tantrum is starting to build. Have a few distraction strategies ready, like offering a favorite toy, singing a calming song, or going for a short walk outside. Distraction shouldn't be used to reward the tantrum. Offer the distraction calmly and gently, and once your child has calmed down, discuss what happened and help them find a healthier way to express their feelings.

- **Ignoring the Tantrum**

This strategy can be effective for attention-seeking tantrums, but it's important to use it carefully and only when you're sure your child is safe. Ensure your child is in a safe environment where they can't hurt themselves or others. Then, calmly acknowledge their feelings but avoid giving them the attention they seek through the tantrum. Experiment with different strategies and find what helps your child calm down and learn to manage their emotions in a healthy way. Most importantly, stay calm and patient – you're doing a great job!

Preventing Tantrums

- **Authoritative Parenting**

Think of leadership styles. Would you prefer a boss who screams or one who patiently lays down rules with a lot of guidance and support? Authoritative parenting is similar. Set clear expectations for your child, but do it with warmth and understanding. Explain the "why" behind rules and offer choices whenever possible. This fosters respect and cooperation, reducing the need for power struggles.

- **Positive Parenting**

Positive parenting encourages desirable behaviors by highlighting them. Catch your child being good and offer praise, like "I love how you used your words to ask for that toy!" This positive reinforcement builds confidence and motivates them to make good choices. Sometimes, when your child throws a tantrum, they just want (although not intentionally) your attention, even if it's negative. Shower them with positive attention throughout the day for good behavior, following rules, and expressing their emotions calmly. This reduces the need for negative attention-seeking behaviors.

Words of encouragement go a long way. Don't underestimate the power of a simple "I'm so proud of you for trying!" Praise effort, not just outcomes.

This motivates your child to keep trying, reducing frustration and potential meltdowns, even when things get tough.

- **Rewards And Consequences**

Set clear expectations about what earns rewards and what leads to discipline and rebukes, like losing screen time for not following rules. Be consistent and avoid empty threats. This helps your child understand what's expected and encourages them to make positive choices. Stick to your established routines and expectations as much as possible, even on challenging days. This creates a sense of security and predictability, reducing anxiety and potential meltdowns triggered by unexpected changes.

Self-Regulation Training

I like to liken our brains to computers processing information at lightning speed. For children with ADHD, this rapid processing can lead to emotional overload. Teach your child to use the "pause button." This could be a physical object, a mental image, or simply taking a deep breath. Encourage them to use this "pause" when overwhelmed, allowing their brain to calm down and assess the situation before reacting impulsively.

- **To Stay Away From Or Take Yourself Out Of Tense Situations**

Children with ADHD often have heightened sensory sensitivities. Help them identify their personal sensory triggers (sights, sounds, smells, etc.) and develop coping mechanisms. This could involve wearing noise-canceling headphones, carrying fidget toys, or taking breaks in quiet spaces. By managing sensory input, they can reduce emotional dysregulation.

- **To Avoid Frustration, Schedule And Prepare Yourself.**

Instead of demonizing frustration, teach your child to view it as a signal, a "frustration monster" trying to get their attention. Encourage them to observe the monster calmly, ask themselves what's causing the frustration, and then choose a healthy response. This could involve expressing their needs calmly, taking a time-out, or engaging in a calming activity.

- **To Alter Your Perspective On Distressing Circumstances.**

Think of reframing as "reimagining" a situation. When your child feels stuck in a negative thought loop, help them look for an alternative perspective. Ask them, "What's the best-case scenario? What's the worst-case scenario? What's something positive we can learn from this?" Shifting their focus from negativity to possibility helps them to manage their emotions more effectively.

- **To Create Fresh Reactions To Rage.**

For children with ADHD, there will be detours in the form of major obstacles, triggering frustration. Teach them the importance of "Plan B." Brainstorm alternative solutions to potential challenges, like carrying extra pencils in case they forget, having calming activities packed for long waits, or practicing relaxation techniques before potentially stressful situations. By having backup plans, they feel more prepared and less overwhelmed.

Chapter Takeaway

- Tantrums alone are not diagnostic of ADHD. Many children without ADHD experience tantrums. However, children with ADHD are more likely to experience more frequent, intense, and longer-lasting tantrums compared to their peers. Different areas of your child's brain can manage things like focusing, controlling feelings, and processing information.

- Intense emotions can be a big blessing but can sometimes feel like a curse. Children with ADHD experience joy, excitement, and love with great intensity. But the flip side is that negative emotions like anger, frustration, and sadness can feel overwhelming and difficult to manage.

- So, bottom line: Your kid's not a 'bad' kid, and you're not a 'bad' parent. No one's to blame for ADHD. Blaming yourself or others and trying to fix things with criticism won't help. Tantrums aren't about being "bad" but symptoms of the underlying challenges associated with ADHD.

- Children with ADHD often have heightened sensory sensitivities. Help them identify their personal sensory triggers (sights, sounds, smells, etc.) and develop coping mechanisms. This could involve wearing noise-canceling headphones, carrying fidget toys, or taking breaks in quiet spaces. By managing sensory input, they can reduce emotional dysregulation.

We have seen the key differences between typical tantrums and those experienced by children with ADHD, highlighting the role of intense emotions and sensory sensitivities. We also emphasized the importance of self-compassion and understanding, moving away from blame and focusing on building a supportive environment.

Now, with a clearer understanding, it's time to move forward and build a positive foundation for growth. This next chapter focuses on the importance of setting clear expectations and rules. Rules and boundaries are not meant to be punitive measures but rather a way to provide your child with structure, predictability, and a sense of security.

9

MASTER THE IMPORTANCE OF CLARITY AND SETTING SIMPLE RULES

"Every game has rules. Life's a game that has its respective rules; obey the rules, and win the game!"

—— *Israelmore Ayivor*

*B*oys and rules often have a complicated relationship, sometimes feeling like a constant clash. For boys with ADHD, breaking the rules isn't always defiance; it's just his way of processing and interpreting the world around him. Their natural curiosity and love of exploration can make rules feel like fences blocking really cool stuff.

Also, processing information and remembering details can be quite difficult, making rules seem like complex puzzles with missing pieces. "Sometimes you can climb, sometimes not?" Confusion and frustration set in. In this chapter, I will show how to recognize your boy's perspective on rules so you can move beyond frustration and create a space where rules can be adaptable and not restrictive fences.

Case Study

From the moment he woke, his mind buzzed with a million buzzing ideas, each more exciting than the last. Unfortunately, the world around him seemed drawn in shades of gray, governed by rigid lines and quiet expectations. The school felt like a constant battle against an invisible enemy: The Rules.

The "sit still" rule was almost an impossibility. Who likes to sit when there are a zillion things to do at the same time? Yet, I didn't like the consequences – stern looks, whispered reprimands, the dreaded time-outs – felt like punishment for simply being himself. "Focus," they'd say as if the focus was a tangible object he could just pluck from the air. He longed to please, to understand, but his brain simply didn't operate in linear, rule-bound ways.

Be Specific

When setting expectations and rules, I like to be very specific about what I expect from my son. For example, instead of saying, "Clean your room," say, "Put your toys in the toy box, your clothes in the closet, and your books on the bookshelf."

- **Use short and direct language**

Keep your instructions short and to the point. Use simple language that your child can understand. I encourage parents to avoid using long sentences, complicated words, or robotic commands. Instead, frame expectations as a joint effort: "Let's work together to ensure everyone in the house can move safely. How about walking instead of running inside?" Explain the "why" behind rules in age-appropriate ways, and be mindful of emotional cues.

- **Break down tasks**

Break down large tasks into smaller, more manageable steps. This will help your child feel less overwhelmed and more in control. For example, instead of asking your child to "clean the kitchen," break it down into smaller tasks like "wash the dishes," "wipe the counters," and "sweep the floor."

If movement helps him stay focused, incorporate short physical breaks into the tasks. You can also use picture charts or color-coded schedules. You can also use methods like chunking information, kinesthetic learning activities, or multisensory reminders. Your goal should be to make tasks achievable and build confidence.

- **Provide examples**

Give your child examples of what you expect. For example, if you want your child to speak respectfully to others, give them examples of respectful language like "please" and "thank you."

Visual demonstrations are helpful, but avoid generic examples. Connect examples to your child's interests and experiences. While using visual aids with my son, I used a picture of a boy giving a toy to his friend. That worked much better than a generic picture of sharing. Use role-playing scenarios that reflect their real-life situations. This personalization resonates better and makes expected behavior more relatable.

- **Use positive language**

Use positive language when setting expectations and rules. Instead of saying, "Don't run in the house," acknowledge potential difficulties: "I know running feels fun, but walking inside helps everyone feel safe. Remember, you can run outside later!" This validates their feelings while reinforcing the rule. Offer alternative outlets for their energy, like jumping jacks or running in designated areas.

- **Involve your child in setting rules**

Involve your child in setting rules. Ask them what they think is fair and reasonable. This will help your child feel more invested in the rules and more likely to follow them. Start with age-appropriate choices for consequences and rules. Involve them in brainstorming solutions, but provide clear boundaries and guidance.

Focus on Key Behaviors

- **Identify the most critical behavior**

Every child has some traits they need to work on. Don't get me wrong, I am not saying every child has bad behavior, but some traits need quick, thorough work. Identifying the most critical behaviors is a foundational step in managing ADHD in your child. Begin by closely observing and noting behaviors that significantly impact daily life at home and school. Common examples include impulsivity, hyperactivity, and difficulty with sustained attention.

You may notice certain behaviors stand out more than others. Take note of these, as they could be the key areas needing attention for your child's well-being and development.

- **Keep the number of rules manageable**

Keep your son focused on the most important behaviors to avoid overwhelming your child. This way, they can better grasp and adhere to your rules. To create a positive environment for your child, keep the number of rules manageable. Setting too many rules can be overwhelming and counterproductive. Instead, concentrate on a few essential rules that address the critical behaviors identified earlier. This approach makes it easier for your child to understand and follow expectations.

- **Prioritize behavior modification techniques**

This is one technique I have found to be super helpful. Behavior modification techniques are really important in managing ADHD. Prioritize techniques that are proven to be effective, such as positive reinforcement, consistent consequences, and structured routines. Tailor these techniques to address the specific behaviors you've identified as most critical for your child. Explore behavior modification techniques like positive reinforcement and consistent consequences (touched on earlier). These strategies can be customized to suit your child's needs, making it more likely for them to respond positively.

- **Regularly review and adjust**

Stay actively involved in your child's journey. I know it's easy to get carried away with dealing with the condition that you may actually lose sight of your son. Review the strategies in place regularly and be willing to make adjustments. You need to be flexible in addressing your child's evolving needs and ensuring continued progress.

Managing ADHD is a journey that involves evaluating and adapting strategies. It's important to assess your child's progress and the effectiveness of the approaches being used. Stay open to making adjustments and modifications as your child grows and develops, as what works for them now may need to be tweaked in the future.

- **Seek professional guidance**

It's completely fine to seek assistance. Please don't hesitate to seek guidance from professionals. Healthcare providers and educators have insights and support to offer. By collaborating with them you can develop a rounded plan that addresses your child's needs.

It's crucial to have guidance when dealing with ADHD. I personally spoke with healthcare experts, educators, and behavioral specialists who provided me with accurate answers and offered support. You can also work alongside these professionals to create an approach that caters to your child's strengths and challenges.

Establish Clear Consequences

Being consistent and clear is very important in helping your child understand the connection between their actions and the outcomes. Here's an example of how you can implement this effectively:

- **Be clear and consistent**

Make sure to communicate the outcomes that come with behaviors. It's important to be consistent so your child comprehends that their actions have consequences. For instance, if they forget to do their homework, you can establish thirty minutes of study time as the resulting consequence. Assist your child in perceiving consequences as an outcome of their actions. Being clear and consistent will aid them in understanding the cause-and-effect connection.

- **Offer choices and control**

Giving your child some freedom to make choices is important as it helps them develop a sense of control. For example, you could let them decide whether to help with the laundry or clear the yard. This way, they'll feel a sense of independence. Also, learn about responsibility and managing their tasks.

- **Time-limited consequences**

You can also make sure that the repercussions for his actions have a time limit and are directly linked to his behavior. Short-term consequences tend to be more impactful and easier for your child to understand. For instance, if they forget their homework, a suitable consequence could be temporarily losing a privilege, such as no screen time for that day. This doesn't imply that you're being harsh. It would benefit you and your son to take a stance on the matter.

- **Regularly review and adjust**

Your child is always developing, so you should regularly assess and modify consequences to match their growth. As they become more responsible, consider adjusting consequences to promote independence and reinforce behaviors. Here's an example of a morning checklist;

Morning routine:

1. Wake up:

    ◦ Set my alarm for the morning.

    ◦ Choose an alarm sound that I like.

    ◦ Place the alarm across the room to help me get out of bed.

2. **Hygiene:**

    ◦ Lay out the toothbrush and toothpaste the night before.

    ◦ Wet my toothbrush.

    ◦ Apply toothpaste.

    ◦ Brush my teeth for two minutes.

    ◦ Rinse my mouth and toothbrush.

    ◦ Dry my face with a towel.

3. **Get dressed:**

    ◦ Choose my clothes the night before.

    ◦ Lay out each clothing item in order.

    ◦ Put on underwear.

    ◦ Put on socks.

- Put on pants.

- Put on a shirt.

- Tie my shoelaces.

- Check in the mirror to make sure I look good.

4. **Breakfast:**

- Get to the kitchen on time.

- Pour cereal into a bowl.

- Add milk.

- Eat slowly and chew my food.

- Clear my plate and put it in the sink.

Actionable Steps to Implement this Strategy

I love to cook, but it can be a little nerve-wracking to start cooking and then discover midway that you do not have one of the key ingredients. Having a plan is like having a recipe for a yummy dish. But for the dish to be complete, you need to gather ingredients and follow the steps. Actionable steps turn your ideas into something tangible, like turning a recipe into a delicious meal. When there's a plan, everyone knows what to do. It helps both you and your child understand your role, making it easier to work together toward a common goal.

Think of it as tracking your journey on a map. Actionable steps help measure how far you've come. It's like marking off places you've visited. Seeing progress keeps you motivated and lets you know you're moving in the right direction. Here are some actionable steps I'm sure will help you to implement this strategy:

- **Clearly communicate the expectation**

Speak directly and clearly about the rules. Imagine you're giving directions to a friend. Use simple words and sentences. Explain why the rules matter, such as saying, "Clean your room so you can find your toys easily."

- **Provide a visual representation of the rules**

Create a visual guide for the rules. Draw or use images to show each rule. This way, your child can 'see' what you mean. It's like giving them a roadmap they can follow with pictures. You can even hang posters with pictures of what you need them to do.

- **Consistently enforce the rules**

Here is the deal: you need to be consistent. If a rule is set, follow it every time. This helps your child know what to expect. It's like making a promise and keeping it. When you're consistent, your child learns that rules are always there. Make sure you use positive reinforcement also. Positive reinforcement is like saying, "Awesome job! I'm proud of you." It makes your child feel good about doing the right thing.

Avoid Approaching The Situation With Anger

I get it; it's so easy to lose your cool. Sometimes, you just want to pull out your hair in anger (and maybe your son's too). However, responding to your child in anger may lead to strained relationships, erode trust, and create an environment of fear. Children may become hesitant to communicate openly, fearing negative reactions. This approach doesn't address the issue's root and can hinder their emotional development. Anger is a storm that passes quickly but leaves behind damage that takes time to repair.

- **Take a moment to gather your thoughts**

You don't have to respond instantly. Taking a moment before responding is like hitting the pause button in a heated situation. This brief pause lets you collect your thoughts and choose your words wisely. It prevents impulsive reactions and allows you to consider the best way to approach the situation. Take a deep breath before deciding the next step.

- **Practice empathy**

I know you might not have the same diagnosis as your child, but you would need to empathize with him. Understanding your child's emotions and perspectives is an aspect of empathy. It's about putting yourself in their shoes and seeing the world through their eyes. When you show empathy toward your son, it establishes a connection built on understanding rather than criticism. This connection strengthens his trust in you further.

- **Control your tone of voice**

The way we speak has an impact on how we communicate. Speaking calmly and confidently creates an atmosphere that makes people feel at ease. On the other hand, getting angry can make your child feel uneasy and defensive. By controlling your tone, you can make sure your message is understood without causing any stress.

- **Focus on the behavior, not the child**

It's important to emphasize addressing the behavior rather than focusing on the child. Just like you can critique a painting without criticizing the artist, separating the action from the person helps avoid assigning blame and enables your child to better understand which specific behavior can be improved. This approach promotes a growth mindset.

- **Offer guidance and support**

Guiding your child in navigating their challenges positions you as a mentor instead of solely an enforcer of rules. This entails aiding them in resolving problems and discovering solutions. By offering advice, you empower your child to make decisions, demonstrating that your role is to foster their development rather than merely penalize errors. This approach nurtures trust, facilitates communication, and fosters respect.

Areas to Avoid

- **Being too lenient**

I had to learn to balance leniency with structure, avoid power struggles, and maintain consistency. While flexibility is important, being too lenient can lead to a lack of boundaries. Your child will do well with clear guidelines and limitations. This will give him a sense of security and an understanding of acceptable boundaries.

- **Power struggles**

Power struggles can also come up when dealing with your child. Avoid turning everyday tasks into contests of will. Instead, try to work together with your son. Make him understand that you are on the same team, not two opposing forces wrestling one another. This approach helps maintain a positive atmosphere where everyone feels heard and respected.

Chapter Takeaway

- Use simple language that your child can understand. Keep your instructions short and to the point. Avoid using long sentences or complicated words.

- Keep them focused on the most important behaviors to avoid overwhelming your child. This will help them better grasp and adhere to your rules.

- Clearly communicate the consequences associated with specific behaviors. Consistency is crucial to help your child understand that certain actions lead to predictable outcomes.

- Responding to your child in anger may lead to strained relationships, erode trust, and create an environment of fear. Children may become hesitant to communicate openly, fearing negative reactions. Anger is a storm that passes quickly but leaves behind damage that takes time to repair.

Now, with this foundation of understanding, let's go into behavioral interventions. This next chapter will give you access to practical strategies to encourage desired behaviors. These are not magic wands but rather effective tools that, when used thoughtfully and consistently, can help your child pull through ADHD.

10

HOW TO USE BEHAVIORAL INTERVENTIONS FOR LONG LASTING SUCCESS

"You have to understand behavior before you can change it."

-Anonymous

*B*ehavioral interventions are really important for boys with ADHD. These interventions teach self-control and organization skills, which makes handling daily tasks easier. This chapter will show you the power of positive reinforcement, which is a big part of these interventions. You will also see how recognizing and rewarding good behaviors helps boys keep doing them. These interventions will help them improve their social skills, making it easier for your son to interact with others and build strong bonds.

Case Study

It took me a while to agree to behavioral interventions. You get to take aspirin for a headache and put on a band-aid for a cut, so why not give my son, Nath, a pill that will make ADHD go away? That was my initial naive hope. Pills seemed like a quick fix, a magic bullet to erase the frustration, the tantrums, the constant feeling of being on edge.

But after weeks of sleepless nights and feeling like I was failing Nath, I knew we needed something more. The pediatrician mentioned behavioral interventions, and while I was hesitant, a desperate part of me clung to the possibility of finding a solution.

It wasn't a transformation overnight. But over weeks, the meltdowns became less frequent and less intense. Nath started expressing his needs calmly, using the "calm down corner" we set up instead of lashing out. We could have conversations, and laughter started filling our home again.

Looking back, I wouldn't trade those behavioral interventions for anything. They really helped—a lot.

Behavioral Therapy

Applied Behavior Analysis (ABA)

Trust me, it isn't as complicated as it sounds. Applied Behavior Analysis (ABA) is like a detective that dissects the "whys" behind actions and uses positive strategies to reinforce desired behaviors. Think of it as giving your son the needed strength for self-control. You can also work with a therapist to identify triggers, analyze their impact, and introduce positive reinforcement techniques like praise, rewards, and token systems.

Positive reinforcement

Positive reinforcement encourages your boy to repeat good behaviors. This technique leverages the power of praise, rewards, and encouragement to motivate positive choices. Positive reinforcement strengthens desirable behaviors. You can develop individualized reward systems aligned with your child's interests. For example, if your boy loves to play video games, you can allow him to play the game a little longer than usual. On the other hand, if he loves to get on a bike and go outdoors, you can allow him to stay out for a little longer. This helps to build motivation and stronger self-esteem.

Self-monitoring

On the other hand, self-monitoring involves teaching your son to become more aware of himself. He learns to identify his triggers (avoid them or work through them, as the case may be). He also learns to track progress and celebrate achievements. Consider it giving him a magnifying glass to zoom in on his identity. You can use self-observation charts, checklists, and apps to help him recognize his behavioral and emotional patterns. This self-awareness helps him to make positive choices and proactively get involved in managing his symptoms.

Behavioral contracts

Behavioral contracts establish clear expectations and rewards for achieving specific goals. These "win-win" agreements can motivate your son to take ownership of his behavior. Just like goals, ensure that these contracts are specific, measurable, achievable, relevant, and time-bound (SMART). You can outline what you need your son to do, the consequences for not doing them, and positive rewards for meeting your expectations. This collaborative approach will help him to be more responsible and trustworthy.

Systematic desensitization

My son gets pretty antsy sometimes, but I've learned that feeling anxious or overwhelmed can be common for boys with ADHD. Systematic desensitization gives you a method for facing fears step-by-step. You can gradually expose your boy to his fears in a controlled environment, starting with low-intensity situations and progressing gradually. He will learn coping mechanisms through repeated exposure and positive reinforcement and build confidence in managing his anxieties.

For example, if your son is afraid of speaking in public, systematic desensitization wouldn't immediately throw him on stage in front of a packed auditorium. Instead, you can start by helping your son visualize himself giving a successful presentation. Then, practice a short presentation in a familiar setting, like your living room, with you playing the audience. You can then expose him to recordings of others giving presentations, starting with short clips and progressing to longer videos with bigger audiences.

With time, you can enroll him in activities like drama club or school projects involving speaking in small, supportive groups. Gradually increase the size and formality of the audience, starting with friendly classmates or a sympathetic teacher.

Contingency management

This might sound complicated, but it's all about cause and effect. Contingency management links actions to their consequences, both positive and negative, helping boys understand the natural flow of choices. Positive choices lead to positive rewards, while negative choices have natural consequences. Establish clear expectations and consistent consequences for both appropriate and inappropriate behaviors. This approach instills accountability, teaches valuable life lessons, and promotes responsible decision-making.

Parent Training Programs

To help your child, you need to stick with strategies learned in training programs. Use them regularly at home for the best results. As I said earlier, consistency is key. Talk openly with professionals, like therapists, to understand how your child is doing and make any needed changes to the plan.

Also, consider combining the parent training with individual therapy for your child. This way, you improve your skills in handling ADHD challenges, and your child gets specific help. It creates a strong and helpful support system for your family.

Parent-Child Interaction Therapy (PCIT)

PCIT helped me and my son a lot. It is designed for kids aged 2-7 and focuses on building a strong, positive connection with your child. Your therapist will guide you through live sessions, teaching positive reinforcement techniques like warm praise and fun games to encourage good behavior. You'll learn to set clear expectations, give effective instructions, and respond calmly even when you are angry. The benefits of this program include reduced tantrums, improved communication, and a more joyful parent-child relationship.

Triple P (Positive Parenting Program)

Triple P will help you find solutions to tackle any parenting issue, not just ADHD. You'll gain practical strategies for becoming a better Mom or Dad with group workshops or individual consultations. The benefits include:

- Improved communication.

- Increased confidence in managing behavior.

- Peace of mind for you and your family.

Parent Management Training (PMT)

PMT equips you with a structured plan to address specific behavioral concerns. You'll learn to identify triggers and understand what triggers the "bad" side of your child. The program emphasizes reward systems, applying positive reinforcement effectively, like rewarding good choices with privileges or fun activities. The benefits include reduced problem behaviors and improved focus and self-control.

Collaborative & Proactive Solutions (CPS)

Yet another big word, but I assure you, it's not as hard as it looks. CPS emphasizes collaboration and open communication within the family. The program focuses on understanding the "why" behind your child's behavior, going beyond just managing it. You'll get involved in problem-solving, working with your child to find solutions that work for everyone. One of the key components of this program is shared responsibility. This ensures that everyone feels heard and involved, thus strengthening your family bond. The benefits include improved communication, increased empathy, and a sense of shared responsibility for going through ADHD *together*.

Cognitive Behavioral Therapy (CBT)

Psychoeducation

Imagine trying to speak French to someone who speaks only Spanish. Tough right? You need to speak and understand your child's language to be on the same level as your child. Psychoeducation in CBT helps you know more about ADHD's impact on your child's cognition, emotions, and behavior. For instance, ADHD might affect attention, memory, organization, and processing speed. This can lead to difficulties following multi-step instructions or staying focused during homework. Knowing these impacts helps you set realistic expectations and makes it easy to work effectively with therapists and educators.

Cognitive restructuring

Negative thoughts fuel negative actions. Cognitive restructuring helps by identifying distorted thinking and challenging unhelpful thought patterns. For example, replace "I'm stupid if I don't get this right" with "Everyone makes mistakes; I can learn from them." It is crucial to encourage your child to question negative thoughts and ask themselves if their thoughts are realistic and helpful. Developing more balanced perspectives, like seeing a challenging task as an opportunity to learn and grow, helps your child develop a growth mindset, reduce self-criticism, and boost their confidence.

Behavioral activation

Overcoming "low motivation" barriers is the focus of behavioral activation. This involves identifying activities your child enjoys, like playing video games or biking. You can start with achievable goals, such as aiming for 15 minutes of reading instead of an hour initially. You can also work toward creating activity schedules to plan time for these activities. Rewarding positive steps, even small achievements, helps your child experience the joy of accomplishment, build positive routines, and combat discouragement.

Emotional regulation

Emotional regulation gives your child an "emotional toolbox." These help them identify emotions by recognizing physical and mental cues, such as feeling hot and tense as signs of anger. Your child will also learn how to develop coping mechanisms, like learning healthy ways to manage emotions through deep breathing, mindfulness exercises, and expressing feelings constructively. Additionally, helping them communicate effectively to express their needs and feelings clearly and calmly empowers your child to manage emotions effectively and reduce impulsive reactions.

Environmental Modifications

Organized and clutter-free spaces

How does it feel to walk into a room so packed you can barely move? Imagine the same room cleared and organized, where everything has a designated place. This simple change can work wonders for children with ADHD who often struggle with visual clutter. Start by tackling one area at a time, involving your son in the process. Let him choose colorful bins or shelves to personalize his space and make it more inviting. Regularly declutter together, turning it into a game or activity he enjoys. This teaches him valuable organization skills while creating a calmer environment that reduces unnecessary sensory overload.

Color coding

Colors aren't just visually appealing; they can be organizational tools for children with ADHD. Assign specific colors to different subjects (blue for math, green for science), chores (red for laundry, yellow for dishes), or even different areas of the house (blue for relaxation, green for homework). Use colored folders, labels, or bins to help your son remember routines, locate items easily, and stay on track with tasks. You can even create a visual schedule using colored charts or magnets, offering him a clear roadmap for the day and reducing confusion.

Noise reduction

I don't like to be in a loud, noisy environment. It's always hard to focus and concentrate. The same goes for children with ADHD. Create designated quiet zones in your home by investing in soundproofing materials like rugs or wall hangings. White noise machines can also be helpful in masking background noises. For individual study sessions, consider noise-canceling headphones or earplugs. You can also work on limiting screen time before bedtime, as the blue light emitted can disrupt sleep patterns and hinder concentration.

Flexible seating

Traditional chairs might not be the best fit for children with ADHD, who often benefit from movement and fidgeting. You can use alternative seating options like wobble stools, exercise balls, or even standing desks. These allow dynamic movement while sitting, helping your son burn excess energy and refocus his attention. Encourage him to get up and stretch, walk around the house, or engage in short physical activities throughout the day. This helps release pent-up energy and refocus the mind, improving concentration and reducing frustration.

Natural lighting

Studies have shown that natural light significantly enhances mood, alertness, and cognitive function. Whenever possible, open curtains and blinds to let the sunshine in. Encourage outdoor activities during the day, as exposure to sunlight helps regulate sleep cycles and boosts energy levels. Invest in bright, adjustable lamps that mimic natural light.

Mindfulness and Relaxation Techniques

Just like your child, you, too, need tools to find calm amidst the chaos. So, take a brief moment for yourself. Close your eyes, take a few deep breaths, and feel your feet grounded on the floor. Notice the rise and fall of your chest and your body's sensations. Acknowledge any stress or tension you might be carrying and gently release it with each exhale. It's going to be alright, you will be fine. Let's move on to how you can teach your son some relaxation techniques.

Deep breathing

Breathing is our most basic life function, but it can also be a powerful tool for calming the mind and body. Teach your son simple breathing exercises like belly breathing, where he places his hand on his stomach and feels it rise and fall with each inhalation and exhalation. Start with just a few breaths at a time, gradually increasing the duration as he gets comfortable.

Progressive Muscle Relaxation (PMR)

This technique involves tensing and relaxing different muscle groups one by one. You start with the toes, clench them tightly for a few seconds, then release. Work your way up the body, focusing on major muscle groups like your legs, arms, neck, and face. This will help your son release his physical tension.

Guided imagery

One other technique I found really helpful is guided imagery. All you need to do is encourage your son to engage his senses and imagine himself feeling calm and peaceful in that imagined space. Guided imagery can be particularly helpful for managing anxiety and promoting relaxation before bedtime.

Mindful breathing

Similar to deep breathing, mindful breathing focuses on bringing awareness to each inhale and exhale. Encourage your son to sit comfortably, close his eyes (if he feels comfortable), and simply observe his breath without judgment. Notice the coolness of the air entering his nose, the warmth filling his chest, and the gentle release with each exhale. This practice cultivates focus and promotes present-moment awareness.

Mindful coloring

Coloring can be a fun and engaging way to practice mindfulness. Provide your son with coloring sheets featuring repetitive patterns or mandalas. Encourage him to focus on the present moment, choose colors intuitively, and observe each stroke's details. This can help quiet the mind and reduce stress.

Chapter Takeaway

- Positive reinforcement encourages your boy to repeat good behaviors. This technique leverages the power of praise, rewards, and encouragement to motivate positive choices.

- To help your child, you need to stick with strategies learned in training programs. Use them regularly at home for the best results. Talk openly with professionals, like therapists, to understand how your child is doing and make any needed changes to the plan.

- Imagine trying to speak French to someone who speaks only Spanish. Tough right? You need to speak and understand your child's language to be on the same level as your child. Psychoeducation in CBT helps you know more about ADHD's impact on your child's cognition, emotions, and behavior.

- How does it feel to walk into a room so packed you can barely move? Imagine the same room cleared and organized, where everything has a designated place. This simple change can work wonders for children with ADHD who often struggle with visual clutter. Start by tackling one area at a time, involving your son in the process.

- As your son transitions into his teenage years, his challenges may evolve and intensify. While the mindfulness and relaxation techniques you've instilled would help him throughout his life, being an adolescent or parenting one requires additional strategies. The next chapter is about the unique challenges teenagers with ADHD encounter, equipping you with practical approaches to navigating academic pressures, social dynamics, and emotional fluctuations.

11

PROVEN STRATEGIES TO WADE THE WATERS WITH YOUR TEENAGER

Adolescents are not monsters. They are just people trying to learn how to make it among the adults in the world, who are probably not so sure themselves.

-Virginia Satir

*T*he teenage years can be quite a ride, filled with changes and self-discovery. It can be exhausting for parents who haven't learned how to navigate this phase. When you add the challenges of having an ADHD teenager, it can become downright scary. Fear not! Navigating through your ADHD teen years doesn't have to feel overwhelming. In this chapter, I'll provide you strategies to anticipate the hurdles you might encounter during this period in your child's life. These strategies will help ensure they receive the needed support and guidance as they transition into adulthood.

Case Study

I once worked with a couple named Maria and John, who had a son named Pete. Pete was diagnosed with ADHD at an early age. His parents have since learned to encourage his creative pursuits despite his struggles with organization, meeting deadlines, and impulse control. But when he started high school, these challenges seemed to intensify. Homework often turned into last-minute studying sessions fueled by energy drinks and constant anxiety *buzzing. His once-jovial fidgeting became outright disruptive, and that caused him to get noticed and increased his frustration.*

As social interactions became more complex, Pete's impatience often led to disagreements that made him feel isolated and misunderstood.

John and Maria also felt the strain. Despite their love for their son, they often felt powerless and exhausted from the arguments revolving around chores, homework, and impulsive decisions. The playful strategies and open communication techniques that were effective in elementary school seemed inadequate to handle the turbulence of puberty.

Hormonal Changes and ADHD Symptoms

ADHD itself can be challenging to manage. However, when you add the turmoil of adolescence into the mix, it's like adding fuel to the fire. Let me explain further.

Puberty and brain development

Every individual experiences puberty—a phase in life when testosterone and estrogen take center stage in altering our bodies and minds. These hormones also influence our brain cells' interactions and development (Hwang et al., 2019). While this "neurological rewiring" is necessary for adult growth it can be unsettling for those with ADHD.

Impact on neurotransmitters

Our brains rely on chemical messengers called neurotransmitters to communicate between cells. Neurotransmitters, like dopamine, serotonin, and norepinephrine, influence mood, attention, and impulsivity. Hormones also play a role in regulating these neurotransmitters. Research suggests that certain hormones, such as estrogen, can affect dopamine levels, potentially worsening concentration issues in individuals with ADHD (Banerjee et al., 2022).

Increased impulsivity and risk-taking behavior

As a result of all these neurological activities, it's not surprising that impulsivity can become a challenge for adolescents with ADHD during this period. When emotions run high, maintaining focus and making judgments becomes difficult. Given the risk of engaging in behaviors like substance abuse or unprotected sex due to impulsivity, guidance and support from parents and educators are essential.

Regular monitoring and communication

So, how can we best assist teenage boys with ADHD in navigating through this rollercoaster of hormones and development? Open communication and regular monitoring are key. It is important to help them recognize when things are not going well and make adjustments. Educators and parents can fulfill this responsibility by:

Tracking symptoms: Monitor how hormonal fluctuations impact ADHD symptoms. Are there any patterns of increased impulsivity or mood swings?

Open communication: It is crucial to create an environment where open and honest conversations about challenges and experiences can occur.

Collaborative strategies: Working collaboratively with your boy, you can develop coping mechanisms and strategies to manage impulsivity.

Emotional Regulation and Mood Swings

It's important to explore techniques that promote positive emotional well-being when it comes to regulating and managing mood swings.

Teach emotional awareness

One of the first steps is fostering awareness. Encourage your son to recognize and label his emotions. Tools such as mood trackers, emotion wheels, or journals can be valuable during this process. Remember to provide validation and understanding while refraining from passing judgment. Creating a space free of judgment for discussions is highly crucial (Price et al., 2022).

Implement relaxation techniques

It is vital to have relaxation techniques readily available when emotions run high. Some examples include muscle relaxation, yoga, mindfulness meditation, deep breathing exercises, and simply listening to calming music. Encourage practice and allow individuals to explore what works best for them (Healthline, 2021).

Encourage artistic expression

Not only is creativity enjoyable, but it's also an effective means of expressing emotions. Sometimes, your teenager can feel overwhelmed and out of control. However, he can find an outlet for those emotions through activities like writing, singing, drawing, or playing an instrument. Supporting and encouraging pursuits is important by providing the materials and opportunities to unlock this invaluable resource.

Offer a safe space for communication

For emphasis, creating a space for communication is vital for well-being. You should strive to establish an environment where he can freely share his feelings without fearing judgment or criticism. Whenever your teenager opens up, it's important to listen by reflecting on what he's trying to say, repeating his words back to him to validate his feelings, and asking open-ended questions that show empathy and understanding. Remember that offering advice isn't the first goal; instead, focus on providing support and being there as a listening ear.

Limit stimulant intake

While medication plays a role in managing symptoms of ADHD (Attention Deficit Hyperactivity Disorder), it's essential to be mindful of the side effects of stimulants. Stimulants such as caffeine, nicotine, and sugar can worsen dysregulation by causing anxiety, irritability, and mood swings. Encourage your teen with ADHD to limit or avoid these stimulants, especially before bedtime. Opt for healthier alternatives like water or herbal tea, or enjoy some fresh fruit instead. It's worth noting that even certain ADHD medications may have side effects; therefore, consulting with a doctor is crucial in determining the best dosage and timing for optimal benefits while minimizing unwanted side effects.

Increased Independence and Responsibility

Every teenager desires to gain independence and take on responsibilities. However, as parents or guardians, we might hesitate to let them spread their wings due to the challenges that come with the years. It's important to remember that keeping them confined at home won't be beneficial. There are strategies you can employ to empower your ADHD teens, fostering a sense of responsibility and confidence while ensuring their well-being.

Gradual independence

Like teaching a child how to ride a bike requires patience; fostering independence in teens with ADHD requires a patient approach. Start with tasks they can easily handle and successfully complete, gradually increasing the complexity and responsibility as they show mastery. For example, you can begin by assigning responsibilities such as setting the table or organizing their backpack.

Clear and simple instructions

When giving instructions, it's crucial to be clear and concise. Teens with ADHD may struggle with understanding instructions, so long lectures or vague expectations won't be helpful. Instead, provide directions in a straightforward manner. If a task seems complicated, break it down into segments that are easier for them to manage. Additionally, visual tools like printed reminders or checklists can aid in improving their comprehension.

Establish routines

By creating routines, you can support your ADHD teen in developing his independence while nurturing responsibility and confidence. For teenagers with ADHD who often thrive on having a routine, it's important to create a sense of predictability and security. Establish bedtimes, waking up times, and times for getting ready for school and completing homework. Encourage their participation in creating these routines to foster a sense of ownership and commitment.

Use of timers and alarms

Another common challenge faced by teens with ADHD is struggling with time management. To address this, introducing timers and alarms can be really helpful. Encourage them to set reminders for managing homework, chores, screen time limits, and other activities. Be sure to acknowledge their progress with positive reinforcement whenever they make improvements.

Encourage self-advocacy

It is incredibly valuable to give teenagers with ADHD the tools to advocate for themselves. Teach them how to recognize their challenges and effectively communicate their needs. Engage in role playing scenarios where they can practice asking for considerations or seeking clarification in social settings.

Risk-Taking Behavior and Impulsivity

It can be difficult to navigate the challenges that come with risk-taking and impulsivity in youngsters diagnosed with ADHD. We know these symptoms might result in potentially dangerous situations, which greatly worries parents and teachers. So, how do we equip these young minds with the tools they need to make safe and responsible choices?

Educate and raise awareness

Awareness and education are the first steps. Using age-appropriate language and examples from real life, have an honest and open discussion about the possible repercussions of their behavior. Assist them in seeing how their impulsivity may impair their judgment and cause them to make poor judgments (Barkley, 2013).

Develop and reinforce rules

While teens crave autonomy, clear and consistent rules provide a crucial framework for decision-making. Collaborate with your teen to establish clear expectations for behavior, focusing on specific actions rather than vague generalities. Ensure that the consequences for breaking these rules should be fair, consistent, and age-appropriate (Barkley, 2013). See these rules as guiding their choices without stifling their independence.

Implement delayed gratification techniques

One hallmark of ADHD is difficulty waiting for desired outcomes. Delayed gratification techniques can help teens develop impulse control and make more thoughtful choices. Encourage activities that require waiting, like saving for a desired item or participating in sports requiring delayed rewards. Celebrate their successes in resisting immediate gratification, reinforcing the value of patience and planning.

Develop coping strategies

When faced with tempting or risky situations, teens with ADHD need effective coping strategies. Teach them relaxation techniques like deep breathing, mindfulness exercises, or counting to ten before acting impulsively. Role-playing scenarios can help them practice using these strategies in real-life situations, building confidence and resilience.

Involve the adolescent in rule-making

Teens are more likely to follow the rules they helped create. Involve them in the rule-making process, discussing potential risks and consequences together. This fosters a sense of ownership and responsibility for their choices.

Parent-Adolescent Relationship

Adolescence itself is a period of intense change and emotional volatility, and for families touched by ADHD, the challenges can feel amplified. Let's examine some strategies to foster connections built on understanding, respect, and collaboration.

Empathetic understanding

You have to cultivate empathy! You must understand that teenagers see the world in a different light, and you might not always have the same perception of things. However, you can ease the strain by actively listening to their concerns, validating their emotions, and trying to understand their unique perspective (Sears & Barkley, 2014).

Educate both parties

Open communication is essential, but it requires a shared understanding. Educate both yourself and your teenager about ADHD. Discuss its symptoms, challenges, and strengths together. Resources like books, websites, and workshops can equip you both with valuable knowledge, fostering compassion and reducing frustration.

Shared decision-making

Teenagers want independence, but managing their lives while they have ADHD may be difficult. As an alternative to imposing regulations, include them in joint decision-making. Talk about what's expected of you both, and the possible outcomes, and together, come up with solutions. This strengthens the relationship by fostering a sense of accountability and ownership.

Establish routines together

Routines give teenagers with ADHD the much-needed structure and regularity they require. Establish regular schedules for going to bed, getting up from sleep, doing chores, finishing homework, and relaxing together. Know that adaptability is essential, preserving a general framework for stability while making necessary changes.

Respect privacy

Adolescence is a time for boundary-setting and self-discovery. Respecting their privacy is as vital as keeping an eye on their well-being. Establish unambiguous guidelines for communication, personal space, and technology use while maintaining a healthy balance between safety and trust. Always keep in mind that communication is essential; foster an atmosphere where people feel at ease approaching you with issues.

Express love and affection

Even during challenging times, expressing love and affection is vital. Behind the impulsive behaviors and emotional outbursts lies a young person who needs your love and support. Offer physical affection, words of affirmation, and quality time spent together, even if it's just enjoying a quiet meal or watching a movie. Let them know they are loved and accepted unconditionally.

Chapter Takeaway

- Hormonal fluctuations during puberty can exacerbate ADHD symptoms, making emotional regulation, focus, and impulse control even more challenging. Understanding this interplay is crucial for supporting adolescents effectively.

- The adolescent brain is still undergoing significant development, impacting areas crucial for attention, decision-making, and emotional processing. Recognizing this ongoing development helps us approach challenges with empathy and patience.

- Imbalances in neurotransmitters like dopamine and norepinephrine can contribute to ADHD symptoms. Medication and behavioral interventions can help address these imbalances and improve overall functioning.

- Increased impulsivity and risk-taking behavior are common concerns. Open communication, clear expectations, and collaborative rule-making empower adolescents to make responsible choices while fostering their independence.

- Regular communication and monitoring are essential. Create a safe space for open dialogue, actively listen to concerns, and work together to address challenges. This builds trust and strengthens the parent-adolescent relationship.

- We explored strategies for managing emotional dysregulation, emphasizing emotional awareness, relaxation techniques, artistic expression, and open communication. Remember, patience, support, and validation are key.

- Fostering gradual independence builds responsibility and confidence. Utilize clear instructions, routines, and timers, and encourage self-advocacy to equip adolescents with the skills they need to thrive.

- Building a strong, supportive relationship is crucial. Cultivate empathy, educate both parties, involve adolescents in decision-making, respect privacy, and express love and affection unconditionally.

12

How to Optimize Physical Activities and Simple Exercises for Your Child

"Physical fitness is not only one of the most important keys to a healthy body; it is the basis of dynamic and creative intellectual activity."

– John F. Kennedy

*B*oys are usually a powerhouse. They have an infectious enthusiasm that can light up a room and bring a smile to everyone's face. However, keeping up with this energy can be frustrating, especially when they are constantly moving.

Engaging in exercise can benefit your son as it helps release pent-up energy and improve focus. It affects the mind while simultaneously strengthening the body. Physical activity enhances blood circulation to the brain, supplying it with oxygen and essential nutrients that enhance concentration and facilitate learning.

In this chapter, we will explore how optimizing physical activity can impact your son's overall well being.

Case Study

It took me some time to understand why TJ always seemed relaxed after riding his bike. When he would return home, there was always a smile on his face like it was glued there. Initially, I thought it was the air, and also, exercises are beneficial for anyone, right? Then, I started noticing this phenomenon in situations.

After playing soccer in the park, he would fall asleep soundly as a rock. After wrestling with our goofy retriever, he would focus intensely on building with Legos. The more he engaged in physical activity, the calmer he appeared. Curiosity sparked within me, leading me to delve deeper into this matter. As it turns out, I wasn't alone in my observations.

Studies have been praising the benefits of activity for children with ADHD. They discuss focus, improved control, and even better sleep as potential outcomes. It wasn't about tiring him out (although that was definitely a bonus). There was something at play here.

I wish I had realized this connection sooner, and I wish I had recognized earlier how physical activity unlocked a side of TJ's personality. However, it's never too late to uncover insights.

Exercise and the Brain

Engaging in activity ensures that the brain has the necessary resources and structure to operate optimally, resulting in long-term advantages for your child's cognitive growth, emotional welfare, and overall well-being. Here are several ways in which exercise positively impacts the brain.

- **Blood flow**

Engaging in exercise causes the heart to beat faster, resulting in better blood circulation throughout the body, including the brain. This surge of blood brings a supply of oxygen and glucose, which are the main sources of energy for the brain. It's like providing fuel to every neuron ready to boost our thinking abilities, learning capacity, and memory. Research has shown that even brief periods of activity can greatly enhance blood flow to the brain, ultimately leading to improved performance.

- **Blood vessels**

Physical activity boosts blood circulation and enhances the intricate network of small blood vessels in the brain known as capillaries. These capillaries play a role in supplying nutrients to brain cells. By exercising, these capillaries remain supple and healthy, ensuring a smooth and efficient distribution of resources throughout your son's brain. It's like establishing an effective transportation system within the city of the brain, enabling seamless information flow. Additionally (for you), stronger blood vessels provide defense against decline and age-related brain conditions.

- **Brain activity**

Research indicates that physical activity stimulates the release of brain-derived neurotrophic factor (BDNF), a protein responsible for promoting the growth and development of neurons. Consequently, this results in enhanced connections between brain cells, thereby improving learning abilities, memory retention, and overall cognitive performance.

More Reasons to Exercise

Trust me, there are benefits to engaging in physical activity. Exercise impacts neurotransmitters, which are the brain's chemical messengers responsible for influencing our mood, focus, and attention. We can increase our dopamine levels through exercise, leading to mood and decreased stress levels. Additionally, exercise helps regulate norepinephrine, another neurotransmitter that plays a role in enhancing focus and attention. This ultimately leads to concentration and learning abilities. Let me share more compelling reasons why you and your child should prioritize exercise.

- **Stay at a healthy weight**

Too much weight can have negative effects on your boy's developing body, raising the chances of heart disease, stroke, and certain types of cancer. It can also worsen sleep apnea, causing disruptions to his sleep and overall well-being. Just imagine having an exhausting day followed by a restless night. Regular exercise will help him burn calories and maintain a healthy weight, reducing the strain on his body and minimizing the risk of future health issues. Moreover, exercise provides an energy boost that can lead to making the right food choices in the future, establishing an early cycle for managing weight effectively.

- **Maintain normal ranges for cholesterol and blood pressure**

High "bad" cholesterol and low "good" cholesterol can clog his arteries, raising the risk of future heart problems. Similarly, high blood pressure stresses his developing heart and blood vessels. These risks are particularly concerning for boys with ADHD, as they may have a higher genetic predisposition. Physical activity naturally improves his cholesterol profile by increasing "good" cholesterol and lowering "bad" cholesterol. It also strengthens his heart and improves blood vessel function, helping regulate blood pressure and reducing the need for medication.

- **Reduce the risk of diabetes**

If diabetes is not managed properly, it can cause issues such as nerve damage, vision problems, and even the need for amputations. Although genetics do play a part, it is crucial for your son to maintain a healthy weight and engage in physical activity to prevent these complications. When your child exercises, his body becomes more efficient at using insulin, which helps regulate blood sugar levels and reduces the risk of developing type 2 diabetes. This is particularly important because even a slight increase in blood sugar can exacerbate symptoms of ADHD.

- **Improve self-confidence and self-esteem**

Feeling good about himself is important for any child, but with ADHD, having healthy self-esteem goes a very long way. They struggle and sometimes endure being put down by adults who do not understand. This can chip away at their self-esteem, impacting their social interactions and overall well-being.

Exercise releases endorphins, natural mood elevators that enhance his happiness and accomplishment. Achieving fitness goals, like running laps or learning a new sport, builds his confidence and competence. Additionally, managing ADHD symptoms through exercise helps him to participate more actively in life, fostering positive social interactions and building self-esteem.

Easy Exercise Ideas for Kids with ADHD

You must ensure that your son does not see exercise as a punishment. It is a good way for your boy to strengthen his muscles, improve flexibility, and boost his confidence. On the other hand, your son might see it as boring and just another item to check off the list. So, how do you get your son to actively exercise and not see it as another grand effort by Mum to frustrate him?

- **Dancing**

Dancing is a fun way to burn excess energy, improve coordination, and boost mood. It engages multiple brain areas, enhancing focus and memory. Plus, it allows for self-expression and creativity. So, turn up the music. Let your son choose his favorite tunes and encourage free movement. You can even join in for bonding time. Explore different styles like hip-hop, breakdancing, or even classical ballet for variety. You might even consider local dance classes for structured learning and social interaction.

- **Martial arts**

Martial arts combine physical activity with mental discipline, improving focus, self-control, and respect. They teach valuable skills like self-defense and build confidence. Research local martial arts studios offering programs for children with ADHD. Look for instructors experienced in working with kids. Start with trial classes to find the right fit for your son's interests and personality. And you can even get started with one or two classes online.

- **Simple yoga techniques**

Yoga offers a calming counterpoint to excess energy. These simple poses improve flexibility, strength, and body awareness. It also teaches mindfulness techniques that help manage impulsivity and improve focus. Find kid-friendly yoga videos online or enroll in a local children's yoga class. Start with basic poses like mountain, tree, and child's pose. Encourage deep breathing exercises and mindfulness practices.

- **Nature walk**

Nature walks provide a change of scenery, promoting relaxation and focus. Fresh air and sunshine boost mood and reduce stress. Exploring nature can also encourage his curiosity and creativity. You can start with trails or parks suited for your son's age and ability. Make it interactive by identifying plants and animals, collecting leaves, or playing nature scavenger hunts. Pack healthy snacks and drinks for breaks. You will definitely need that.

- **Hula-hooping**

Have you ever heard of hula-hooping? It is a fun and active way to improve coordination, balance, and core strength. It's a low-impact activity that can be done almost anywhere. Choose a hula hoop that's the right size for your son's height and skill level. Practice basic moves like waist rotations and figure eights. You can learn more advanced tricks online or through instructional videos. Make it a family activity and have fun hula-hooping together.

Get Out of the House

Stepping outside exposes you to fresh air and natural sunlight, which have numerous positive effects. Fresh air promotes better concentration and reduces stress, while sunlight provides essential vitamin D for strong bones and a healthy immune system.

Leaving the house also encourages physical activity, whether walking in the park, riding a bike, or playing at a playground. This helps combat sedentary lifestyles, especially for boys needing more active outlets.

- **Have a picnic**

Picnics will help you relax and also set a tone for conversation and laughter. This strengthens your father-son bond (or mother-son bond, as the case may be. Pack a variety of healthy and delicious snacks and meals to make it a fun and nutritious experience. Picnics can be simple or elaborate, depending on your preferences and time constraints. They're perfect for a quick lunch break or a full-day outing.

To get started:

1. Look for parks with picnic tables, playgrounds, or open spaces for frisbee or ball games.

2. Consider locations like lakes, beaches, or botanical gardens for added beauty.

3. Check for amenities like restrooms, playgrounds, or walking trails if desired.

Fun things to do:

- Play frisbee, soccer, or other outdoor games.

- Go for a nature walk or explore the surroundings.

- Read books together or tell stories.

- Do some stargazing if it's an evening picnic.

- Build a sandcastle or play in the water if you're near a beach.

- **Go camping**

Pitching a tent, cooking over a campfire, and exploring the outdoors together create lasting memories and strengthen your relationship. Camping exposes your son to new environments and teaches valuable skills like teamwork, problem-solving, and outdoor survival. You also get to unplug from technology and daily routines, allowing you to unwind and appreciate the simple pleasures of nature.

Choose a campground that suits your experience level and desired amenities (e.g., showers, swimming pool, on-site activities). Consider guided camping programs or tours for beginners or those seeking a structured experience. Look for campgrounds with activities like hiking, fishing, or kayaking if you want to explore the surroundings.

Fun things to do:

- Go hiking or explore nature trails.

- Build a campfire and tell stories or roast marshmallows.

- Do some stargazing and learn about constellations.

- Go fishing or swimming (if allowed at the campground).

- Participate in organized activities offered by the campground.

- **Visit a museum**

Museums offer a wealth of knowledge and experiences to help spark your son's imagination. You can choose museums that align with your son's interests, whether dinosaurs, art, history, or science. Museums challenge thinking skills and encourage critical thinking as you explore exhibits and discuss them together. You also get exposed to diverse cultures, historical periods, and artistic expressions, broadening your understanding of the world.

Fun things to do:

- Participate in interactive exhibits or workshops offered by the museum.

- Play museum scavenger hunts or trivia games to make learning fun.

- Draw or write about your favorite exhibits to solidify your memories.

- Discuss the exhibits and what you learned with your son.

How to Help Children With ADHD Sleep

I like my beauty sleep. Though I guess it has more to do with getting my stuff together than "beauty." When sleep-deprived, it is usually harder to concentrate. Now, imagine how that's going to be for a boy with ADHD. Adequate sleep fuels the brain, enhancing cognitive function, memory consolidation, and information processing. This translates to better focus in school, improved learning, and sharper performance in various activities.

I try as much as possible to get a good night's rest because sleep deprivation can wreak havoc on anyone's mood, making them irritable, impatient, and prone to emotional outbursts. This is especially true for boys with ADHD, who may already struggle with emotional regulation. Getting enough sleep promotes emotional balance, reduces impulsivity, and improves their ability to handle stress and navigate social interactions more effectively.

Boys with ADHD often have overactive minds that struggle to switch off. Ruminating thoughts, racing ideas, and a general difficulty quieting down can make falling and staying asleep challenging. Even when their bodies are tired, their brains might still buzz with activity.

They may also experience heightened sensory sensitivities. Lights, sounds, or even the feel of their sheets can be distracting and disruptive, making it difficult to relax and drift off. External factors like traffic noise or siblings' late-night activities can exacerbate this.

So, how exactly do you get your son to sleep?

- **Addressing the child's needs before bed**

Ensure your child gets enough physical activity during the day, but avoid vigorous exercise close to bedtime. Encourage calming activities like reading or light stretching in the evening. You can also work on limiting sugary foods and caffeine throughout the day, especially in the afternoon and evening. Offer a light, healthy snack before bed if needed. More importantly, reduce exposure to screens, especially those with bright blue light emission, at least an hour before bedtime. Opt for calming activities like reading or listening to audiobooks.

- **Reducing anxiety and dependence on caregivers**

Teach your child mindfulness exercises like deep breathing or progressive muscle relaxation to unwind before sleep. Consider guided meditations specifically designed for children. If your child relies heavily on your presence to fall asleep, gradually increase their independence. Start by sitting near them as they drift off, then slowly move further away over time. Talk to your child about their worries and anxieties related to sleep. Address them with patience and understanding, offering reassurance and support.

- **Establishing a healthy sleep environment**

If needed, create a dark and quiet sleep environment using blackout curtains, earplugs, or a white noise machine. Ensure the room temperature is cool and comfortable, ideally not too cold or hot. You can check with your son to confirm a comfortable temperature. Choose soft, breathable bedding and a supportive mattress.

- **Maintaining a consistent routine**

Establish a regular bedtime and wake-up time, even on weekends, to regulate their internal sleep-wake cycle. Create a relaxing bedtime routine that includes calming activities like taking a bath, reading a story, or singing a lullaby. Stick to the same routine every night to signal to their body that it's time to wind down. Avoid stimulating activities like playing games or watching TV close to bedtime.

- **Implementing sleep hygiene**

While some nap time may be necessary, long or late afternoon naps can interfere with nighttime sleep. Encourage regular physical activity throughout the week, but avoid strenuous exercise close to bedtime. Ensure your child drinks plenty of water throughout the day, but avoid excessive fluids close to bedtime. Limit caffeine and sugary drinks, especially in the afternoon and evening, as they can disrupt sleep.

Chapter Takeaway

- Exercise gets the heart pumping, increasing blood flow throughout the body, including the brain. This surge delivers a vital dose of oxygen and glucose, the brain's primary energy source.

- Excess weight puts a strain on his growing body, increasing the risk of heart disease, stroke, and even certain cancers. It can also worsen sleep apnea, further disrupting his sleep and overall health. Imagine dealing with a busy night after a much more busy day.

- You have to ensure that your son does not see exercise as a punishment. It is a good way for your boy to strengthen his muscles, improve flexibility, and boost his confidence. On the other hand, your son might see it as boring and just another item to check off the list.

- Sleep deprivation can wreak havoc on anyone's mood, making them irritable, impatient, and prone to emotional outbursts. This is especially true for boys with ADHD, who may already struggle with emotional regulation. Getting enough sleep promotes emotional balance, reduces impulsivity, and improves their ability to handle stress and navigate social interactions more effectively.

You've done an amazing job reading so far. It's clear how much you care about your child and are dedicated to helping them thrive. That's truly inspiring. Now, let's get on to the final chapter of this book, which is all about you.

While we've focused on supporting your child, you need to note that your well-being is equally important. Taking care of yourself isn't just self-indulgence; you must be the best version of yourself for your child and your family. In the next chapter, we'll explore practical ways to stay positive and healthy so you can approach each day with freshness.

13

LEARN TO STAY HEALTHY, POSITIVE, AND RELENTLESS

"It is not how much we have, but how much we enjoy that makes us happy."

– Charles Spurgeon

*S*elf-care doesn't just mean spa days, girls' night out, dads' only fishing trips, or even date nights. Sure, those things recharge our drained batteries, make us feel human, and give us much-needed respite. But they don't help us to manage the worries, anxiety, frustration, anger, sadness, and any other range of emotions that come along with being an ADHD parent. It is not a luxury to cram between doctor's appointments, school meetings, and soccer practice. Self-care really means taking the time to prioritize your own needs in every role you play: not just Mom or Dad, but partner, worker, friend, family member and more. It means engaging purposefully in acts designed to promote physical, mental, or emotional well-being.

This last chapter is about self-care and beautiful words you need to stay positive and healthy even while dealing with the heartaches that come with ADHD.

Case Study

Helen surveyed the wreckage of her living room. Toys spilled like lava from a volcano, cushions lay scattered like fallen soldiers, and the faint aroma of burnt toast clung stubbornly to the air. Her reflection in the dusty TV screen was a haggard mess, mirroring the chaos around her. "Total mess," she muttered, not just about the room, but about herself.

Raising her son, Tony, was tough. Dealing with his ADHD often left her feeling like a deflated balloon, her own needs ignored in the face of his constant demands. There were days when the only "self-care" she managed was a stolen sip of cold coffee and a five-minute shower with the bathroom door locked. But the guilt gnawed at her. She knew, deep down, that a frazzled, depleted Mom couldn't be the best Mom for Tony.

Stay Positive

Keeping a positive outlook amidst the chaos can feel like an uphill battle, but you need it to maintain your sanity and your child's. Here's how you can cultivate positivity in each aspect of your life:

- **Maintain a positive attitude**

Start small. Begin your day with a gratitude practice. List three things you're grateful for, big or small. This simple act sets the tone for positivity. You also need to rebuke negative thoughts. When negativity creeps in, catch yourself. Reframe the thought into a more positive or realistic one. "My child is struggling, but they're also incredibly resilient and determined." No matter how small, acknowledge and celebrate your child's (and your own) achievements. This reinforces positive behavior and builds confidence.

As I said earlier, seek out supportive friends, family, and online communities who understand your journey. Their encouragement can be a powerful boost.

- **Keep things in perspective**

Don't get discouraged by setbacks. Focus on long-term progress and not just the small "defeats." Compare yourself to your own journey, not others'. Every child and family is unique. Comparing your situation to others will only lead to frustration. Focus on your own progress and celebrate your unique strengths.

Even amidst chaos, there are always positive aspects. Take time to appreciate the good moments, big and small.

Laughter truly is the best medicine. Find humor in the everyday chaos, and share it with your child. Trust me, it's a good way to relieve stress and build connections.

- **Don't sweat the small Stuff**

Dear Dad/Mum, pick your battles. Decide what truly matters and let go of the rest. Is that forgotten homework assignment worth a meltdown? Probably not. Both you and your child are learning and growing. Don't get bogged down by striving for perfection. Take a deep breath. When you feel overwhelmed, take a few minutes to breathe deeply and center yourself. It helps you approach situations with a calmer perspective. You might also need to forgive yourself and your child. Everyone makes mistakes. Forgive yourself and your child for setbacks, and move forward.

- **Believe in your child**

Every child with ADHD has unique talents and strengths. Help them discover and nurture these strengths, building their confidence and self-esteem. Also, be your child's cheerleader: Let them know you believe in them, no matter what they go through. Your unwavering support is a big plus to them. Embrace their unique quirks and perspectives. They bring a special light to the world; don't dim it. Be patient; change takes time. Be patient with your child and yourself, and trust that progress is happening, even on the days it feels invisible.

Self-Care

Again, self-care isn't a luxury; it's a necessity. So, let's go over some essential practices to replenish your reserves and face each day with renewed energy and strength:

- **Seek support**

You probably have heard the saying, "Life is better when we do it together." As cliche as that statement may be, it has so much value and truth. You may feel alone, exhausted, and sometimes hopeless as you walk through your parenthood journey. Know that you are NOT alone! There are so many others dealing with similar parenting struggles. Part of finding help in these struggles is discussing them and working through them with a community. Encouragement from a partner, friend, family member, or support group who understands will help you to feel heard, seen, and ready to begin each day empowered.

As a parent, If you are having a hard time finding those who are on the same parenting journey as you, try searching for a support group in your area. If there are no groups nearby, several private support groups on Facebook and Instagram are accepting new members.

- **Take breaks**

Give yourself a break. Whatever that means to you, do it. Whether it is sleeping in, having a spa day, going to yoga or for a long walk, working on your mindset, journaling, or working with a life coach or counselor, know that being loving and supportive of yourself is one of the best things you can do for your self-care as a parent. Parenting is the hardest job out there, and I commend each one of you who shows up with the best version of yourself

- **Take care of yourself**

Taking care of yourself is essential, not only for your health but also to have the energy to maintain positivity for your child. Your positivity is what will help your child's strengths to excel in all environments

- **Eat right**

If you're a parent with a kid who has ADHD, you might not realize how important it is for you to eat healthy foods. After all, your child is the one with the condition, so it's easy to focus on making sure they're eating right.

However, it's also important for parents to model healthy eating habits. A nutritious diet can help improve focus and concentration, which are essential for managing ADHD.

Additionally, healthy foods provide the energy needed to keep up with an active child. And finally, by eating well yourself, you'll set a good example for your child to follow.

- **Exercise**

As a parent, it can be tough to keep up with a kid with ADHD. It feels like they're always on the go, and it can be hard just to keep up, let alone try to get them to focus on homework or chores. But it's important to find time to exercise, even if it's just a little bit.

Exercise releases endorphins, which can help improve your mood and focus and promote healthy brain function. When you're more focused and have more energy, you'll be able to better parent your kid with ADHD.

Stay Organized

Smart organization strategies can create a calmer and more predictable environment for yourself and your child. Here are some things you can do to help you reclaim control and conquer the chaos:

- **Create a family calendar**

Invest in a large, visible calendar (paper or digital) accessible to everyone in the family. This becomes your command center for appointments, activities, deadlines, and special events. You can also use color codes (we discussed that earlier). Use different colors for each family member's activities, school events, and reminders. This helps everyone quickly visualize their schedule and identify potential conflicts. Block out time slots for morning routines, homework, meals, extracurricular activities, and bedtime. This creates a predictable structure that helps everyone stay on track. Use calendar apps that sync across devices and allow for reminders and notifications. Consider apps with features like shared calendars, color coding, and task assignments.

- **Establish routines**

Create a consistent morning routine for everyone, including set wake-up times, breakfast rituals, and getting-ready steps. This predictability reduces morning stress and helps everyone start the day smoothly. Establish a dedicated time for homework, chores, and free time after school. This helps children transition smoothly from school to home and sets clear expectations. Use a relaxing bedtime routine with calming activities, screen-free time, and a consistent sleep schedule. This promotes better sleep hygiene for everyone.

- **Use checklists**

Create daily, weekly, and monthly checklists for individual and family tasks. Break down large tasks into smaller, manageable steps to avoid being overwhelmed. Have pre-made checklists for packing lunches, sports bags, and vacation suitcases. This reduces last-minute scrambling and ensures everything gets included. Keep a running grocery list on your phone or fridge to avoid forgetting essentials. You can use online shopping and delivery options for added convenience. Create a chore chart with age-appropriate tasks assigned to each family member.

- **Prioritize and delegate**

Not everything is urgent. Learn to differentiate between urgent and important tasks. Prioritize essential tasks and delegate or postpone less critical ones. Delegate tasks to your partner or children, or even utilize outside resources like cleaning services or grocery delivery. You don't have to do it all alone. Don't overload yourself with commitments. Learn to politely decline requests that drain your energy or time. Encourage your child to take ownership of their responsibilities, age-appropriately. This fosters independence and teaches valuable life skills.

- **Declutter regularly**

Regularly declutter your home to reduce visual clutter and minimize distractions. Donate or sell unused items, and establish designated storage spaces for everything else. Use baskets, bins, and organizers to keep belongings contained and easily accessible. Label everything clearly for easy identification and retrieval. When handling an item, decide immediately if you need it, use it, or discard it. This prevents clutter buildup and saves time in the long run. Involve your child in decluttering activities age-appropriately. This teaches them the value of organization and helps them manage their own belongings.

Develop Coping Strategies

ADHD requires a unique blend of love, patience, understanding, and, most importantly, effective coping strategies. But where do you begin when faced with a mix of emotions, challenges, and daily hurdles?

- **Self-reflection**

Take time for introspection. What are your triggers? What brings you calm? How does your own emotional state impact your interactions with your child? Identifying your strengths and weaknesses is crucial for developing effective coping mechanisms.

Writing down your thoughts, feelings, and experiences can be a powerful tool for self-awareness and emotional processing. It allows you to identify patterns, track progress, and celebrate victories, big and small.

- **Stay calm and positive**

Practice mindfulness techniques like deep breathing, meditation, or progressive muscle relaxation. These can help you center yourself, manage stress, and approach situations calmly.

Let me repeat: when negativity creeps in, don't allow it to stay. Reframe them into more positive or realistic statements. "This is a tough moment, but I've overcome challenges before and can do this again."

- **Establish a support system**

I mentioned this already, but I need to emphasize it again. Find your tribe. Lean on your loved ones: Don't be afraid to ask for help from your partner, family, friends, or even professional resources. Delegate tasks, share responsibilities, and allow yourself to be supported.

- **Flexible parenting style**

Children with ADHD often thrive on flexibility and structure, not rigid rules. Adapt your approach based on the situation and your child's needs. Let go of the pressure to achieve some unattainable ideal.

- **Celebrate small wins**

Redefine what constitutes a "win." Did your child brush their teeth without prompting? Did they complete a challenging task without frustration? Celebrate these small victories. Acknowledge and reward your child's efforts, big and small. Don't forget to celebrate your wins as a parent! Did you stay calm during a meltdown? Did you come up with a creative solution to a challenge? Acknowledge your efforts and celebrate your resilience.

Establish Structure and Stick To It

Let's take a practical approach to this. This mini workbook will guide you through key strategies to implement structure.

- **Strategy 1: Follow a Routine**

A routine gives you a predictable framework to navigate your tasks and responsibilities.

Activity:

1. Identify your key activities: List the essential tasks you need to accomplish daily, weekly, or monthly (e.g., work, exercise, meals, hobbies).

2. Block out time slots: Allocate specific time slots for each activity in your schedule. Be realistic – leave room for flexibility and breaks.

3. Post your routine: Display your schedule in a visible location, like a calendar or whiteboard.

- **Strategy 2: Use Clocks and Timers**

Time management is crucial for sticking to your structure. Clocks and timers will give you visual cues and keep you on track.

Ask Yourself:

- Do I underestimate the time tasks actually take?

- Am I easily distracted during certain activities?

- Can I use timers to incentivize myself during challenging tasks?

- **Strategy 3: Create a Quiet Place**

A dedicated space free from distractions allows you to focus, relax, and recharge.

Activity:

1. Identify a suitable area: Choose a quiet corner, study room, or even a designated nook in your living space.

2. Minimize distractions: Declutter the space, remove devices, and inform others to respect your quiet time.

3. Personalize your space: Add calming elements like plants, soft lighting, or soothing music.

- **Strategy 4: Do Your Best to Be Neat and Organized**

Living in a cluttered environment can add to stress and hinder productivity. Aim for a level of organization that works for you.

Activity:

1. Declutter regularly: Go through your belongings and discard unused items.

2. Designate storage solutions: Use shelves, containers, and organizers to access your belongings easily.

3. Develop cleaning routines: Establish regular tasks to maintain order and avoid clutter buildup.

Ask Yourself:

- What areas of my life contribute most to clutter?

- Does having things readily available help me stay productive?

- Can I create a system for minimizing clutter buildup?

Celebrate Progress

Set Realistic Goals

Instead of a vague "be more organized," try:

- Specific: "Organize your school bag every evening before bed."

- Measurable: "Have all homework folders, textbook, and water bottle packed and ready to go."

- Achievable: Start with 2-3 items and gradually increase.

- Relevant: This helps develop organizational skills they'll use throughout life.

- Time-bound: Give them a 10-minute timeframe to avoid feeling overwhelmed.

Create a Progress Chart

Instead of a regular checklist, you can get creative.

- For younger kids: Use a sticker chart with fun characters or themed stickers (dinosaurs, superheroes, etc.).

- For older kids: Design a progress bar they can color in or use a digital app with customizable rewards.

- Make it interactive: Let them choose rewards and celebrate milestones together.

Celebrate Effort, Not Just Results

Sure, an A+ deserves praise, but what about the struggle?

- Acknowledge the effort: "I saw you studying really hard for that test, and it paid off!"

- Celebrate persistence: "I'm so proud of you for not giving up even though that homework was tricky."

- Reinforce new strategies: "Trying the flashcard method was a great idea. It helps you remember your vocabulary words."

Journal Progress

Rather than just forgetting past victories, create a personal record:

- Encourage them to keep a "success scrapbook": Collect pictures, drawings, or written reflections about their achievements.

- Use a gratitude journal: Prompt them to write down things they're proud of or things that went well each day.

- Review the journal together: Relive past milestones and celebrate how far they've come.

Involve the Whole Family

Make celebration a team effort.

- Plan a family movie night: Choose a movie based on their interests as a reward for reaching a goal.

- Have a themed dinner: Celebrate with their favorite food or cook a dish related to their achievement together.

Chapter Takeaway

- Keeping a positive outlook amidst the chaos can feel like an uphill battle, but you need it to maintain your sanity and your child's.

- You may feel alone, exhausted, and sometimes hopeless as you walk through your parenthood journey. Know that you are NOT alone! There are so many others dealing with similar parenting struggles. Part of finding help in these struggles is discussing them and working through them with a community.

- Sometimes, stress begins with the expectation level we set for ourselves and the people around us. As a parent, your goal is to empower your child to learn and grow at an appropriate pace. Understanding your child's development level will help you set realistic expectations for present and future levels.

CONCLUSION

"*Encourage and support your kids because children are apt to live up to what you believe of them.*"

— Lady Bird Johnson

If there's one thing I want you to take away from finishing this book, it's this: You can be a great parent to your son, ***even if he has ADHD***. This journey won't be easy; there will be bumps along the road and moments when you question everything. But be assured that you have the strength, resilience, and love to build a beautiful, connected relationship with your son.

ADHD isn't a deficit; it's a different way of being. Your son experiences the world with an intensity and vibrancy that others might miss. He sees connections, feels emotions, and approaches problems with a unique perspective. It's your job, dear Mum/Dad, to honor this difference, not erase it.

Throughout this book, we've explored the science behind ADHD and the complexities of emotional regulation, impulse control, and defiance. I have thoroughly discussed evidence-based strategies, from positive reinforcement to active listening, visual schedules, and sensory breaks.

The most powerful tool you have is your compassion. So, go for compassion and not control. Put yourself in your son's shoes. Imagine the frustration of a mind constantly buzzing, emotions surging like waves, and impulses screaming for release. Understanding his struggles doesn't excuse his behavior but allows you to respond with empathy and guidance, not anger and control.

This journey is a marathon, not a sprint, so please focus on progress, not perfection. There will be setbacks, meltdowns, and moments where you feel like you're taking two steps back. Celebrate the small victories, acknowledge the effort, and remember that progress, not perfection, is the goal. Be patient with yourself and your son, and trust that even the stumbles lead you closer to a stronger, more connected relationship.

Build your village. Look for support from communities, professionals, and other parents who understand the joys and challenges of raising a child with ADHD. Share your experiences, learn from others, and build a network to lift you up during tough times. This "village" is not meant for your child alone; it's also meant for you.

The most important part of parenting is "you." You need to take care of your physical and emotional well-being. Trust me, it isn't being selfish; it's a necessity. Schedule time for activities you enjoy, connect with loved ones, and prioritize your own rest and relaxation. A replenished parent is a better parent equipped to handle the emotional demands of raising a child with ADHD.

Don't let the label of ADHD define your son. Instead, celebrate his unique strengths and interests. Encourage his passions and creativity, and give him opportunities to shine.

Never lose sight of the love that brought you here. Let that love be your compass, your guiding light. Through the laughter and tears, remember how far you have come. I'll end with some affirmations for you and your precious son. I need you to believe every word of it because it's true.

For You:

- I am a strong, capable parent, equipped to handle the challenges of raising a child with ADHD.

- I am worthy of love, support, and compassion, both from myself and others.

- I am a lifelong learner, open to new strategies and approaches that benefit my son and myself.

- I trust my intuition and make decisions that are best for my family.

- I am allowed to make mistakes, and they are opportunities for growth.

- I prioritize my well-being, knowing it fuels my ability to be a better parent.

For Your Son:

- You are uniquely wired, with incredible strengths and talents to offer the world.

- You are brave and resilient, capable of overcoming challenges and achieving your goals.

- You are loved unconditionally, just as you are.

- Your emotions are valid, and you have the right to express them in healthy ways.

- You can learn and grow, and I am here to support you every step of the way.

- Your diagnosis does not define you, but by the amazing person you are becoming.

Repeat these affirmations daily, write them down, and share them with your son.

I am constantly rooting for you!

YOUR FREE GIFT

T his groundbreaking guide not only offers a comprehensive approach to managing ADHD but also includes exclusive, limited-edition resources specifically designed to enhance your parenting strategies and support your son's development in facing his unique neurodevelopmental disorders.

7 FREE BONUS Toolkit for Success!

BOOK 1: Parent's Goal Setting and Personal Development Toolkit

BOOK 2: Parent's Emotional and Cognitive Techniques

BOOK 3: Parent's Daily Management and Tracking

BOOK 4: Neurodivergent Child Emotional and Health Management

BOOK 5: Neurodivergent Child Academic and Daily Planning

BOOK 6: Neurodivergent Child Personal Development and Self-Awareness

BOOK 7: ADHD Behavior Tracker

These toolkits are meticulously designed to assist parents in managing the complex needs of neurodivergent children, supporting sibling relationships, and fostering inclusion in every aspect of life.

Hurry, This Special Offer Is Limited! Secure Your Copy Now! To get access to these bonuses and your **FREE AUDIOBOOK** , scan the QR code below or visit

Get FREE AUDIOBOOK HERE!

If you scanned the QR code and didn't receive the message, feel free to DM me 'FREE AUDIOBOOK' to get your hands on a free audiobook!

THANK YOU

T hank you so very much for your purchase of my book.

You could have easily bought a dozen other books, but somehow you took a chance on this one.

So THANK YOU for getting this book and making it all the way to the end.

Before you leave, there would be one tiny favor that I would like to ask of you. **Could you kindly leave a review on the platform? Posting a review is the best and simplest way to support the work of independent authors like me.**

Your feedback will help me continue with the kind of writing that will help you get the results that you wanted. I will highly appreciate hearing from you.

>> **Leave a review on Amazon US** <<

>> Leave a review on Amazon UK <<

Explore More!

If you enjoyed this book and are curious about more of my stories and writings, I invite you to visit my Amazon author page. Your support means the world to me and helps me continue creating stories you love. **Check out my other books here** and dive into new adventures. Thank you for reading, and happy exploring!

REFERENCES

ADDitude Editors. (2021, April 27). The Trickiest Transitions for Our Kids — and Proven Remedies. ADDitude Magazine.

ADHD and the brain. (n.d.-a). Www.understood.org. https://www.understood.org/en/learning-attention-issues/child-learning-disabilities/add-adhd/at-a-glance-adhd-and-the-brain

American Psychiatric Association. (2013). Diagnostic and statistical manual of mental disorders (DSM-5).

Attention Deficit Hyperactivity Disorder (ADHD) - National Institute of Mental Health: https://www.nimh.nih.gov/health/topics/attention-deficit-hyperactivity-disorder-adhd

Banerjee, S., Kumar, V., & Sengupta, S. (2022). Sex and gender differences in ADHD and their underlying mechanisms. Frontiers in Human Neuroscience, 16, 861209.

Barkley, R. A. (2014). Attention-deficit hyperactivity disorder: A handbook for diagnosis and treatment (4th ed.). Guilford Publications.

Barkley, R. A., & Hinshaw, S. P. (2002). Attention deficit hyperactivity disorder (ADHD) in children and adolescents (2nd ed.). Guilford Press.

Bitsko, R. H., Claussen, A. H., Lichstein, J., Black, L. I., Jones, S. E., Danielson, M. L., Hoenig, J. M., Davis Jack, S. P., Brody, D. J., Gyawali, S., Maenner, M. J., Warner, M., Holland, K. M., Perou, R., Crosby, A. E., Blumberg, S. J., Avenevoli, S., Kaminski, J. W., Ghandour, R. M., & Meyer, L. N. (2022a). Mental Health Surveillance Among Children — United States, 2013–2019. MMWR Supplements, 71(2), 1–42. https://doi.org/10.15585/mmwr.su7102a1

CDC Archives. (n.d.-a). Archive.cdc.gov. Retrieved January 15, 2024, from https://archive.cdc.gov/#/details?url=https://www.cdc.gov/ncbddd/adhd/features/key-findings-adhd72013.html

CHADD (Children and Adults with Attention-Deficit/Hyperactivity Disorder): https://chadd.org/: https://chadd.org/

CHADD (Children and Adults with Attention-Deficit/Hyperactivity Disorder). (2023, January 11). Executive functioning support for kids with ADHD.   Retrieved   from https://chadd.org/attention-article/executive-functioning-support-for-kids -with-adhd/

Effective Effort Consulting. (2023, January 10). Helping middle school kids who struggle with executive functions. Retrieved from https://effectiveeffortconsulting.com/helping-middle-school-kids-who-struggle-with-executive-functions/

Faraone, S. V., Banaschewski, T., Coghill, D., Zheng, Y., Biederman, J., Bellgrove, M. A., . . . Wang, Y. (2021). The World Federation of ADHD International Consensus Statement: 208 evidence-based conclusions about the disorder. Neuroscience & Biobehavioral Reviews. doi:10.1016/j.neubiorev.2021.01.022

Harvard University Center on the Developing Child. (n.d.). Executive function.

Hoge, E. G., & Pelham, W. E. (2017). School-based behavioral interventions for ADHD: A review of meta-analyses. Journal of Clinical Child and Adolescent Psychology, 46(5), 713-734. doi:10.1080/15374416.2017.1300513

Hwang, S., Velanova, K., & Aron, A. R. (2019). Sex hormones and adolescent neurodevelopment: Implications for understanding sex differences in psychopathology. Developmental Cognitive Neuroscience, 39, 91-101.

Inheriting Mental Disorders. (n.d.-b). HealthyChildren.org. http://www.healthychildren.org/English/health-issues/conditions/emotio nal-problems/Pages/Inheriting-Mental-Disorders.aspx

National Institute of Mental Health. (2022, June). Attention deficit hyperactivity disorder (ADHD). Retrieved from https://www.nimh.nih.gov/health/topics/attention-deficit-hyperactivity-di sorder-adhd

National Institute of Mental Health: https://www.nimh.nih.gov/health/topics/attention-deficit-hyperactivity-di s o r d e r - a d h d : https://www.nimh.nih.gov/health/topics/attention-deficit-hyperactivity-di sorder-adhd

Posner, J., Rothbart, M. K., & Sheese, B. (2014). Attention

Price, A., Mitchell, S., Janssens, A., Eke, H., Ford, T., & Newlove-Delgado, T. (2022). In transition with attention deficit hyperactivity disorder (ADHD): children's services clinicians perspectives on the role of information in healthcare transitions for young people with ADHD. BMC Psychiatry, 22(1), 251. https://doi.org/10.1186/s12888-022-03813-6

Sears, W., & Barkley, R. A. (2014). Defiant teens: A parent's guide to understanding and managing defiance and anger problems. Guilford Publications.

Willoughby, M. T., Blair, C., Pelham, W. M., & Marqusee, S. (2004). Developmental trajectories of self-regulation and school outcomes in children with ADHD. Developmental Psychology, 40(4), 591-604.

Made in the USA
Las Vegas, NV
16 July 2024

92393826R00118